CEO'S
INSIGHT ON
SALES
AND
MARKETING

CEO'S INSIGHT ON
SALES AND MARKETING

First edition issued June 1, 2018
English edition issued December 25, 2019

Author: Nam Houn (Patrick) Lee
Translation and Calibration : Eden Um / E-mail. edenum87@gmail.com
Issuer: Seon-Bok Kwon
Editor: Bo-Song Kwon
Design: Bo-Mi Seo
E-book: Bo-Mi Seo

Publisher: Happy Energy
Publication Registration No.: 315-2011-000035
Address: 157-010 Hwagokro, Gangseo-gu, Seoul, Korea 232
Phone: 0505-613-6133
Fax: 0303-0799-1560
Web site: www.happybook.or.kr
Email: ksbdata@daum.net

Price $18.50   ₩22,000
ISBN 979-11-5602-7645   13320

Mentorship From **A CEO**
: Power of **Successful Habits**

CEO'S INSIGHT ON

SALES
AND
MARKETING

Nam Houn (Patrick) Lee

Acknowledgments

I wrote this book to inspire and mentor those navigating through the sales and marketing division of the world of the medical device. We sometimes find ourselves in the stage where we are stalled out, lost and in need of a professional and personal mentor. This book will offer a solution to them.

The Korean version of this book was published last year. Since then, I have accrued three groups of readership.

The first group consists of those who struggle to read and only skimmed the book.

The second group includes CEOs of other companies. They read this book multiple times and provided it to their employees.

The third and final group is those who I intended to address-entry-level employees, passionate employees who are seeking mentors, and overseas employees.

I saw a need for an English version for the English speaking, foreign employees who wanted to learn from this book. I, too, think that the purpose of publishing this piece is not for revenue but education. My wish is that this work becomes a guidance manual for the readers.

One of the oversea employees has read this book multiple times and has actively practiced the lessons. It is rewarding to know that I have influenced even just one employee.

The English version started serendipitously. During a dinner with the American branch employees, I was discussing the contents of the book. Playfully, I asked one of the employees if having an English version of the book would be helpful for the employees of international branches and people in the medical device field. She eagerly agreed and got to work right away on the new version.

I want to acknowledge her work, time, and effort. Third-party translation services may have been an excellent alternate option but would have lacked a depth of understanding that she gained while working as sales for the medical device industry.

During the process of translation, I revisited this book and saw a few points that I wanted to revise. In the one year since the Korean version of this work, my perspective and vision have evolved. However, I still believe that many will benefit from the basics of marketing and sales in this book, and my path to success will inspire and encourage novice journeyer.

I sincerely hope that this book will drive readers to change their lives, improve and build better careers.

Relationship Strategy

PART 3

Marketing and Sales Strategy

Part 1

Task
Handling
Strategy

Smart Time Management

Early in my career, I learned that to stand out in the rigid corporate society of Korea, I had to go the extra mile. Therefore, I worked harder and longer than all of my colleagues.

Each culture is different, and my experience may only apply to the competitive and rigid Korean corporate culture. However, diligence is recognized across all cultures. If you are in marketing or sales, I recommend that you arrive at work an hour earlier than regular hours. You may utilize the extra hour on personal errands and collect your thoughts before beginning the day. There are many advantages to going to work an hour earlier. An obvious one is that you will never be late. To you, the new working hours are 8-6 rather than 9-6. Personally, as a new entry, I always went to work an hour and a half earlier.

People may question if such measures are necessary, and my answer is that the benefits I saw from the extra hour outweighed the discomfort of waking up an hour earlier.

Another advantage is getting noticed by upper management. Quite surprisingly, the majority of executives and upper management start their days early. As your encounter with them becomes more frequent, and they will notice you. You will be seen as a diligent and earnest employee. I do believe that I built a reputation as a dilligent worker because of my early morning encounters. Not surprisingly, industrious employees will generally perform better at work.

You should dedicate the first few years of your career to learning. When an employee comes to work late and takes care of personal errands, drinks coffee, then goes out for a smoke, he will have wasted the entire morning. Many employees who are habitually late may be guilty of not prioritizing work and not having control over their time. A corporation is a place where only the most competent survive. Sacrificing an hour in the morning to better prepare will get you ahead of the crowd. In any fight, the one who strikes first wins.

Strike first and strike hard with your work by showing your boss how well prepared you are. Your boss may not be aware of all your minuscule tasks and requests. By appealing to your boss before anybody else, you may get the privilege of having your request completed before others.

You may have noticed a wanderer who goes from one department to another and spends too much time getting coffee or chatting with others. Though he may seem as if he is wasting time, he may be cooperating across different department to reach the best solution.

Don't let distractions undermine your productivity. Begin the day with an end in mind. Have an expectation that you will get work done on time. A builder needs a blueprint to build a house. Like a builder, have a blueprint of tasks and goal in mind for a successful, efficient day.

For one hour, prioritize your tasks by sorting them into degree of importance and urgency. Imagine the day in your head, and manage the workload on your timeline.

Dedicate an hour of your morning to reflect your goals and purpose for your work. Use the time to evaluate whether you have ownership of your time, and gauge whether you have let others interfere with your time and effort.

Why is it so hard to leave work on time? Staying late at work may be an evidence of negligent time management. Have a rule for what you choose to do with your time. Divide your workload into urgent, important, and menial tasks. Minimize any time wasted by limiting your tasks outside of your proposed work and set aside time for answering emails and making calls.

The key to staying on top of the workload is to find a sensible order of work. Work through the important but not urgent responsibilities first. I also recommend using a planner to track your work and reading books on effective time management.

It's crucial to develop a habit of completing the daily tasks before you leave work. Once the practice becomes a lifestyle, you will have a know-how in managing time according to the workload.

Although this may sound difficult at first, starting the day with the intention of completing the daily workload on time will give you an immense amount of focus.

Confucius once said,

> "*Youth will determine the life plan, Spring will determine the year plan, Morning will determine the daily plan. If you don't learn as a youth, you will not know as an elder, If you have not sown in the spring, you will not see fruit in the spring, If you do not wake up in the morning, you will not have accomplished anything by the end of the day.*"

Treat each morning as a sacred time. If you reluctantly force yourself out of bed and grudgingly come to work, your day will be barely tolerable. Then, your days at work will merely become one of two things: days that you can "tolerate" or days you "avoid."

Work
before the Work

Do you fully comprehend the purpose of the work assigned to you? The goal of the task? Are you ready to answer with confidence on why you have to carry out the assignment?

There is a valued employee at work. He was a bright young man who had graduated from a notable college. However, he didn't have the privilege of working with the best superiors. His work became restricted to what was assigned to him, and he quickly limited himself to just that. Watching his struggle during the transition from one manager to another, I was more convinced than ever to put into writing exactly what any corporate employee must learn on his or her own, with or without a caring superior. One must learn to work out the purpose and reason for the work before he or she begins any task.

Before beginning any work, you must first consider,

- What is the object of this task?
- What is the reason behind the assignment?
- What knowledge and skills are required for this job?
- Who currently possesses such knowledge and skills?
- Are there additional information and tasks that go along with the assignment?
- How will you be evaluated?

If you were to put this into writing, this becomes the statement of work.

To analyze the three-month sales trend by product category, start by answering the six questions above. Just as you need to first work on the blueprint of the house before you can start building the house, you need to plan out the tasks.

Most employees have routines that they follow. They open emails, sign off on a few action items, and then start working on projects. If you, too, are starting each day like this, then you may be meandering through work without a clear purpose and direction. Sometimes, there are urgent emails that can't be pushed aside. However, you may have been squandering your morning hours doing menial tasks far removed from the goals of the company, the team, and yours. I recommend that you practice pondering on the purpose and reason for the work.

Morning comes to everyone but not everyone uses their mornings to properly start the day. How you start each morning will determine how the rest of your day pans out. If you take off in the wrong direction, it will take twice the effort to get back on the right track.

I recommend taking a few hours on a Sunday night to reflect and list unfinished tasks from the prior week and upcoming tasks for the coming week. Each weekend, sort the previous lists to categorize the tasks into completed, incomplete, and in progress. If a task remains in the incomplete list week after week, you should consider delegating the responsibilities to others or omitting the task altogether.

Remind yourself daily of the below points to prepare yourself for an efficient day.

- Monitor the progress of this weeks plan
- Review the daily tasks' time line
- What does the company or boss expect of me?

As I mentioned in the earlier chapter, set aside time during the day for answering emails and calls. Do not let non-urgent emails break the rhythm of the workday. Take the time in the morning to sort through the organized list. Before you turn on the computer, review the weekly, monthly, and quarterly plans and strategize how to allot your time and energy. The key here is to monitor your work progress and to question your motives behind the work. When you stop questioning your work and purpose, you will find yourself going through the motions of work mindlessly and without direction.

The biggest difference between an employee who thrives at work vs. an employee who barely gets by is in how each employee prepares for work. A builder who spends hours planning and framing the work will build the best building. Tackling a project without a plan will not only drag out the process but will make it hard for you to stay engaged. I recommend that all my employees take at least an hour in the day to review yearly, quarterly, monthly, and weekly work goals. Hard work and planning don't guarantee success, but sitting in front of the computer staring at the screen won't be any better. I encourage them to cultivate good work habits for the most efficient work life.

In *How to Enjoy Your Life and Your Job*, Dale Carnegie writes about good work habits:

1. Remove all from your desk things not related to the work at hand.

2. Work in the order of importance.

3. Resolve issues the instant they arise. Do not push off a decision at a later time.

4. Learn to congregate, delegate, and manage work.

Finding Work
Life Balance

Working overtime is not an indication of a productive workday.

What is causing you to work overtime? Do the effects of working overtime manifest themselves to higher productivity? a period one can fully concentrate is relatively short. Working overtime is not an indication of a productive workday.

When I was at Amore Pacific and Daewoong, I often worked overtime. Not because I had to, but because I had yet to discover that few hours of concentration can produce higher quality work than long and stalled hours.

If you were to gather people to go golfing at the crack of dawn, you would find enthusiastic and eager reactions. However, if you were to gather people for work, you would find a disgruntled reaction. Why is it that people are willing to withstand the discomfort for entertainment, which would cost them money, but not for work, which would compensate them?

It may take years, but once you learn to prioritize and witness the outcome of intense focus, you will discover the joy of work. Not all work delegated to you by your boss is important. As you spend more time with your boss, you will develop the trick of discerning which tasks are necessary and which are extraneous.

People tend to believe blindly that constant hard work will translate to success. They often make the mistake of overlooking the direction and timing of their efforts. If you are learning at top speed but are headed in the wrong direction, you will get farther from the goal. Time spent thinking and planning is never time wasted. Steven Covey suggested working with an end in mind. Rearrange your focus to the end for maximum productivity.

What does it mean to work with an end in mind? For instance, when developing a new product, imagine how it will bring in sales. The product specifications, price, and marketing platform will depend on the outcome you want to achieve. Market research will also depend on what you imagine. Use 80% of your time and effort to planning; use the remaining 20% to execute those plans.

Some departments see faster employee turnover rates than others. Team members of such departments find work arduous, lengthy, and continuous. Even with overtime, the workload does not decrease much.

The inability of the department to decrease the workload for its members is evidence that the department has yet to implement a working system and is instead relying on manual labor. Customers will find it difficult to trust the products of Samsung if it resorted to manual production.

The ultimate goal is to convert every operation to a systematic function. I had witnessed the change in the dynamic of operation when we implemented ERP across all operations. Human error was down to 1% after just five months. A well-functioning system will change the culture of the company. By reducing redundant and menial tasks, employees can invest their time and energy into more productive and innovative work. Upper management is responsible for identifying ineffective systems. Although transitioning to a new system may take significant time, it will ultimately increase the productivity level of the employees.In the mean time it can temporarily call for longer hours and more work for the employees.

It's crucial to evaluate the reason for the overtime. The long hours you put into work will ultimately pay off. Evaluate how your time is spent, and what you are spending it on. If you find that you are working long hours on doing menial tasks, you may be working under an inefficient system or guilty of unproductive time management.

Preparing Project Proposal

The initial stages of a project include a planning phase and presenting of the plan. Ideally, you need to understand the work before beginning the processes, but realistically, most of the time, you are rushed into a project and have to give a report unexpectedly.

Most entry levels will not have enough skills to create innovative plans for the project and will resort to following the orders of the leaders. We are programmed to follow precedents rather than create new solutions.

Let's change the paradigm on reports. Believe that your report will impress others. Create a report that sets your work apart from others. We often fall into the trap of thinking that our responsibilities are just orders from our bosses. Each new project is a new opportunity and a ticket to your success.

Your window to success opens up each time you make a lasting impression on others.

And opportunity is everywhere. The key is to develop the vision to see it. Athletes think of each game as an opportunity to prove themselves. We need to adopt such a mindset; your reports will display your reluctance and frustration with work. Strive to impress others with your report! Your reports must be designed to get others to agree with you.

Try including the following points:

- Objective and Purpose
- Goal
- Procedure

- Budget

- What is the competitor doing?

- Why do we have to execute the project?

- Why would the customer say yes?

- Design and development resource planning

- Who is the most qualified personnel for this job?

Organize your reports around the above points. It will simplify your report. Then consult with a mentor for expert opinion. Seek colleagues' and potential customers' opinions on how persuasive your reports are. In seeking out ideas, do not limit yourself to people with whom you are cordial, but, instead, reach out to those with whom you are uncomfortable.

Your boss and the upper management will be interested in how your report was received. Inform them on how the customers and others responded to your report. Lay out the advantages and disadvantages of the project and convince them of why the project should head in the suggested direction.

Though this process may be unfamiliar to you in the beginning, after a year or two of interacting with your boss, you will have the mindset of leadership and present the necessary components.

Reports are not daunting tasks. Out of the human population of seven billion, ten percent are of similar educational levels, and ten percent out of them will have had similar dilemmas as you. In other words, your report will not consist of all new ideas but rather a compilation of previous research organized in a logical manner. A corporation needs workers who tackle reports as an opportunity to win over people and to grow into persuasive and influential leaders. Inform the leaders how the customers and others responded to your report, layout the advantages and disadvantages of the project, and convince them of why the project should go in the suggested direction.

Though this process may be unfamiliar to you in the beginning, after a year or two of interacting with your boss, you will have the mindset of the leadership and ease through the reports.

Importance of
New Ideas

How do we find new ideas? How do the sales force and marketing team come up with new ideas when they are not part of the R&D?

Do all ideas succeed? How does a design stand out? Production and manufacturing have to be in place before an idea can come to fruition. Market research with a prototype will tell you how the customers will receive a product. Testimonies from a sample of customers who have used the prototypes will affect the next model of the prototype. After numerous versions of the prototype, the final product needs to acquire registration from the governing health agency.

Each step requires funding. Even after the registration, marketing costs, operating costs, and sales support charges will follow. Imagine you are on a bike, if you stop pedaling the bike will stall and you will eventually fall. Life cycle of a product is similar to a bicycle. Once an idea comes to life and becomes a product, the operation team cannot stop pedaling to keep the product afloat. The new product will have to fight off competitors, patent rights, and more to survive in the market. The market is a battlefield.

The battlefield varies widely for medical device companies, depending on the safety grade of the products. Governing health agencies classifies medical devices by safety grades and require different criteria and testing for each class.

To increase sales in such a place, the company needs to introduce innovative and groundbreaking new products. Expanding the market share and adding indications may help with sales, but the life of a medical device company relies heavily on new product development.

Manufacturing companies are in dire need of new products. Distribution companies, such as Amazon, rely on manufacturers for new products. Unfortunately, a new product doesn't always bring in revenue. The innovators may feel a sense of pride in what they have accomplished, but the reality is that their original work may draw no attention from the market and cease to exist. There are very few products that survive after the initial market launch. Then, how can we guarantee that a new idea will evolve into a lucrative product? How did the rich become rich? Did they suddenly wake up with a great idea? The best selling products were, in fact, an enhanced version of existing products.

Not everyone lives to think about launching a revolutionary product. The fastest and easiest way to achieve a market innovation is to find a way to cost effectively produce an enhanced version of a working product. It's safe to say that Korean medical device companies came into existence in such manner. Most Korean products are reasonably priced with the best value but are not premium brands. The current status is concerning, but that is the truth of the Korean market.

We need to start somewhere and begin with an existing idea. Then approach the medical device field and collect the necessary data. In foreign countries, there are quite a few physician-owned companies. These physicians see a need for improvement in their practice and develop a product to address the need. HansBiomed is focusing on creating products that address the needs and areas of improvement felt by the end-users in the medical field. New product ideas exist in the operation room. An idea starts with observing difficulties the users face with the existing product.

At first, your product may be a mere copy, but by

adding on such ideas and improving the product, you will have a more efficient and effective product that can be used more widely. If you succeed in resolving the need, then you will have created a new innovative product that is set apart from the competitors' offerings.

There is a phrase that says, "There is nothing new under the sun." I disagree. If you persevere and persist, new opportunities and new ideas will present themselves to you. Ideas spring from wanting to create something new and better. Marketers for companies like J&J and Hansaem spend little time in the kitchen with homemakers. They observe the women's daily routines and locate areas that call for improvement. As a medical device marketer and working in sales, you should spend time in the operating room to come up with new ideas to help improve their practice. Ok pyo Joun writes in his book, '*Winning Habit:*'

"*Imitating a role model is a strategy. Don't be*

shy about doing so. Find the best role model for benchmarking."

Imitate the behavior and habits of a leader in your field. Imitation will eventually lead to discovering your method of success.

You are at the starting line. Where you launch off to is in your hand. Start following the path created by a well-respected leader in your field and ultimately have the goal of taking over their position. That will be your winning habit.

Self-Development at Work

We spend a good portion of our lives trying to improve ourselves mentally, physically, emotionally, and even intellectually.

In the workplace where learning may not be so readily available, how can you pursue higher learning? I want to encourage you to pick up reading. Simply put, the more you learn and input information into your mind, the greater the quality of your output. Books are the most accessible form of knowledge and, unlike on-line gossips and tabloids, may hold the answers to the questions and dilemmas of humanity regarding money, success, happiness, and health. I follow the wisdom of Schopenhauer[1], Nietzsche[2], Stephen Covey[3], and Pomnyun[4]. The more I sought after their wisdom, the more my thoughts and actions reflected their teachings. Often these philosophers, thinkers, and activists depict their hardships and their paths to success in their written works. I find that I grow through reflecting on how they championed turmoil in their lives.

Computer skills, certificates, and additional languages are all skills that can enhance your performance. Having skills that differentiate you is important. For several years, I attended workshops and educational seminars that the Department of Labor hosted. It was refreshing to learn something new through these classes, rather than sleeping in on the weekends. I found joy in collecting various certificates.

- - - - - - - - -

1 The philosopher of Germany, worked on private author

2 The philosopher, pioneer of existentialism

3 A business scientist, author of 'The 7 Habits of Highly Effective People'

4 Zen master of Korea

It feels like we have an eternity, but time will not present itself to you for long. You may have heard of the common phrase that there is a time for everything. It's especially true when it comes to studying and working. Getting your foot in the corporate door is just the beginning. Start enjoying the time you have at work; devise how you can make your time here more pleasant, and you will experience a fulfilling life.

- What are you capable of?
- What are you not capable of?
- How does a highly successful person approach a task?
- What do I need to do a better job?

Let's first begin by identifying the areas you are struggling with.

Consider the four points while you learn about the precedents and contemporaries. We are living in a world of lifelong learning, so it may be helpful to find a running mate to motivate you to continue to learn. Having a running mate will make it easier to stay disciplined about investing time for learning and will encourage you to keep up with their pace.

Reading and reviewing are a real skill set. If you are not constantly challenging your brain by reading and reviewing material, it will be that much more difficult for you to pick up new information. You are responsible for upgrading your intellect. I encourage you to continuously read and study to better equip yourself for any role ahead.

The Real Reason for Anger

It's natural to feel angry at work at times. However, what is the reason for your anger? Do you think you won't feel angry at work if you were to selectively do only the things you enjoyed? You must first learn the root issue behind your anger in order to find out the answer.

The main source of frustration at work is in the interactions with people. People are not likely to agree with you on the direction/vision you have for a task. Vajiramedhi[5] writes in his book, '*Happiness is Here and Now*'

- - - - - - - - -
5 The Zen Master of Thailand and Bestseller Author

"Anger will destroy your accomplishments and drag you into a dark pit. If you are continue to nurture such malignant being, I would like to impose a question to you, is there anyone else more foolish than you?"

I do not proclaim to know all the answers; however, I may be able to help you find the reasons for your anger.

First, your expectations may be too high. Your customers may have no intention or potential, but yet because you think that you have a strong relationship with the customer, you assume that the customer will purchase from you. Don't expect to attain their trust overnight. It takes time for them to give you their complete confidence. Before you can climb Mt. Everest, you will need physical training and should seek out advice from experienced hikers.

The second reason is impatience. You are eager to see the work to its completion, so when you stumble upon

hurdles, you grow impatient. I live by the philosophy of "never give up." Success depends on more than good strategy, skill sets, and abilities. Success comes to those who persevere and endure all circumstances when others give up. There is no need to feel despair. Rather than being anxious whenever you are faced with difficult customers, transactions, or issues, remind yourself that you are in it for the long haul. In any negotiation, the party who has more room to maneuver will come out on top. Anxiousness is a mere feeling. Before you feel compelled to give up, suppress your anxiety and take a step back to view the bigger picture. Byung Kwon Koh said in his book 'Philosopher and Maid '

> "Anxiety is a sin. The unfortunate person suffers
> from time. Anxiety prevents you from staring at
> the problem. The impatient person cannot see the
> progress of the problem sufficiently, so he wants to
> consider a substitute as a solution to the problem."

The other party will easily detect your anxiousness
and will see through your lack of preparation. You will
appear like an amateur.

Those who are anxious hold on to one-dimensional
solutions that ultimately cannot resolve issues at hand.

What can we do to take a laid-back approach to a
problem? We have to develop the skill of taking a
step back to look at the broader picture of a problem.
Imagine the potential outcomes of your actions, the
direction, and the progress of the work. Imagine what
a successful resolution will look like and enjoy the
process. At the end of the process, you will have earned

a valuable experience, and such a strategic desire to grow will motivate you.

I have heard a lot of complaints from employees that their hard work is not recognized. Management may view and evaluate your work differently. To minimize the discrepancy of opinions, I advise basing the evaluation of performance on quantitative scale.

There are a lot of questions that shed light on this inherent conflict. "What have I achieved through this work? What are the qualitative and quantitative outcomes of this work? If you are in sales, how many accounts have you added vs. how much deeper is your relationship with an account? Are you working to your full potential? Are revenues, profits, and market share increasing?" Assess your performance based on concrete data. Sales is a very logical and scientific field. Be wary of becoming complacent with your performance based on how hard you think you have worked.

Are you stuck in a rut with no exit in sight and no progress? The problem will not resolve itself before you begin any work. Foresee the potential problems that may arise and prepare to adapt and face the changed conditions. Don't wait for others to find the solutions. Any salesman who elude problems will not be around for long.

Those who are quick to respond and quick to adapt will get to the finish line. Your proficiency will depend on how quickly you plan and execute action items. People who wait around for issues to pass them, who look for the easy way out, and who get angry at the new problem all have one thing in common: laziness. The laziness provokes anger, a passive attitude, and denial.

Dale Carnegie suggests how one can tackle fear in his book Personal Development.

< Fighting the good fight against fear >

1. Write down what you are worried about.
2. Write down what you can do about it.
3. What will you do about it?
4. Put it into action.

"Pondering too long on whether you are happy or not is the shortcut to becoming unhappy. Don't waste your time wondering if you are happy. Live life fully and keep yourself busy. Prevent yourself from falling into the swamp of misery by focusing on the activities rather than your thoughts."

Key Differences Between
A Manager and a Team Member

Team members will have individual goals for carrying out the assigned responsibilities. It is the team leader's role to collect the individual goals to meet the goal of the company.

While the employees may complain about work and the company, a good leader will not partake in such talks. Leadership is not based on how well you can sympathize with the members but how well you can resolve their complaints and worries and create a positive working environment for them.

Some members of the team are unwilling to accept

their shortcomings and will blame others. Such attitudes are noxious to the work environment. It is the leader's job to readdress such members and align cooperation among the members.

A leader must become the mediator between the company and the members. Delineate the goals from the perspective of the members and assist them in translating the goals into their own terms.

The team leader must research and understand the background of the work and help the team members collaborate on working towards a common goal.

For instance, before you can assign new employees to work on a deal with a company, you must first get them to understand the reason and the benefit of the desired transactions.

Here are few points that can help you deliver the correct information to the members:

- Correlation between new Locations and Sales Expansion

- Increased sales through new locations (other teams, organizational cases)

- Comparison table with team members who worked in charge with other team members

- Why we need new places in the long run

- List of new clients that can be challenged now

As mentioned before, it's important to discuss the reasoning and purpose of the tasks with the team members. A leader's job is not to merely pass along information. Do not pass along information from the management without reviewing them yourself first. Take time to organize the data to be comprehensible to members. Without this effort and preparation, you will spend more time discussing the data. Every day, week, month, quarter, year, analyze the data by:

Sales Trend by Customer/ Exit Customer Trend /

Sales Trend by Item / Increase in new accounts /

Overall AR collection /

Sales of newly launched products / VIP management status

For a new hire to become a team manager, if you've never managed employees, you can't manage teams or departments. You have to go through all kinds of people in your organization and gain experience.

If a team leader is promoted without spending enough time with the team members, the new team, no matter how well-worked, will be overwhelmed by their position and role in the company. Naturally, there will be disagreements between the people around and below. A team leader must not forget that he can only achieve his goals with the works of fellow employees. Raising and growing people may seem slow at first glance, but the organization with the best cooperation will win.

As noted above, the first and foremost role of a team leader is to know and direct the work accurately, and to be an assistant to help employees move, according to the strategy to produce predicted results. New important factors are a morally clean fund execution, fair rules, and a respectable personality. It may be difficult in the beginning, but after overcoming hurdles with your team, you will get to taste the true excitement of work. After many successes and failures, you will gradually rise to a business manager or an executive position.

Effective
Meeting Method

We sit in on numerous meetings. Meetings can be a place for employees to discuss their inputs, produce constructive guidance for the team and unite them toward a clear goal. But there are also meetings in which no one gains anything because the management is too busy criticizing the performance of the team.

There are a few basic rules for meetings that must be met in order to achieve the maximum results. In any meeting the main rule is that all attendees understand the reason for the meeting.

In other words, we have to clearly understand the goal

and purpose of the meeting. By a week before, a day before, and three hours before the meeting, everyone attending must share the same understanding of what the meeting has been called forth to accomplish. After the goal and purpose are shared, check the following:

- Is it a routine meeting or a spontaneous meeting?

- Who are the attendees, and do all of them understand the reason for the meeting?

- Are the core members who can contribute to the meeting present?

- Who is going to present, and who is going to aid in explaining?

- People will lose focus after two hours. What is the time limit?

- Will you be discussing throughout the meeting or at the end?

- Did you review the topic and discussion for the meeting? Who reviewed the contents prior to the meeting?

- Have you organized the issues and results from the previous meeting?

- What is the progress of the action items from that meeting? Were the tasks designated to the responsible personnel?
- How are the responsibilities distributed?
- Who is going to oversee the progress until the next meeting?

You may find it difficult to address the above points for the first few meetings but after enough practice, you will have far more effective and productive meetings. Everyone's time is valuable, and you may not get the same members together again, so you can't be negligent about preparing for a meeting.

I recommend having a fixed schedule for the meetings to avoid any schedule conflicts. Having a set date will also remind the owners of the meeting to follow up with the twelve points above prior to a meeting.

Managers and upper management should get involved

in scheduling and running the meetings rather than leaving it up to the entry-levels. The attendees should clearly comprehend what roles they must play in the meeting and what they can contribute.

Don't pass up on an opportunity to attend board or management meetings. These meetings will help you perceive the perspectives of the leadership, You have to think like a leader to become one. Hard work and long hours alone will not make you a leader.

Before starting any meeting, discuss the progress of action items from the previous meeting. Eight out of ten people feel that meetings are unnecessary and are quick to dismiss action items from a meeting. Designate an owner of a meeting who can oversee the meeting and keep everyone one focused on following through the action items. Meetings will go to waste if the action items from the previous meetings are incomplete.

Meetings are the basic and essential means for a

group to gear toward better outcomes. Minute thoughts can congregate to a grander result under the right environment. For entry levels and rising stars, meeting time is where they can shine and display their passion and abilities.

Meetings are not a tedious and unnecessary step at the workplace but rather a time for you to share your goals and tasks for the team and gain assistance to complete the projects.

Also, you have to be transparent about sharing the mistakes and stumbling blocks. Many of your coworkers and superiors will have gone through issues and will gladly lend a hand if you seek their advice. But if you hold on to your problems until the end, then it may be too late.

Contrary to what you may believe, the best way to gain trust to move up the corporate ladder is by showing the good as well. People have a tendency to flaunt what they are good at and hide their shortcomings. Others are quick to evaluate your true abilities, and so you are more likely to gain trust by openly admitting your needs and discussing your problems. Let them help you and learn from their experiences.

Achieving
the Vision

What is a vision? People often cite "difference in vision" or "lack of vision" for leaving a company.

A vision reflects a promise of the future and not the current situation. For example, someone who has accumulated two-thirds of the fund needed to purchase a house can visualize buying a house, but a person deep in debt will have a hard time grasping such a vision. A clear vision helps you pursue dreams and achieve goals. A vision that is clear will open your mind to the endless possibilities of the future.

Then, what vision can you hold on to as an entry-level

employee in a marketing or sales position? What is your personal vision? What is the vision of the company?

A vision for a corporate employee falls into three general categories: promotion, raise, and incentive. A clear vision for success enables you to divulge your skills and abilities and collaborate with others to propel you forward on your journey. Along the path to fulfilling the vision, you will discover the joy in great team work and recognition.

We receive evaluations and incentives at the end of the year. A company rewards those who performed with a raise and incentive.

The well respective, and high performing employees did not become successful overnight. They went through years of experience. For an entry-level employee, it's important to asses what they can do in the current situation to gain the most experience and learn the skillsets to develop momentum towards success.

Do not be quick to be discouraged when your own strategies fail. Seek out a vision model at work It takes perseverance and tenacity to adhere to a vision against the prospect of failure.

Your ultimate goal is to surpass your role model. Learn the equations for success that they previously solved and add to your own set of means to success.

Everything I learned at various levels of position have helped me in my path towards success, in starting my own company, to becoming one of the youngest CEOs in the field. I only began to dream of starting my own company just three months prior to leaving the last company. From an entry-level to an assistant manager position at Daewoong and the sales director position at DN company, I only envisioned the success of the company.

I would not have been able to adhere to my vision of succeeding in the company if I had let obstacles influence my walk. Years of perseverance and endurance compounded my success in starting and managing my own startup.

From the moment you start at the company to the time you resign, set your vision to becoming the best at your workplace. Find joy in the work that you do and discover your abilities and fortes. If you can find a manager who appreciates your work and compensates you accordingly, invest your all into propelling to the top for the next three, five, and ten years. After that, success will find you wherever you are. Vision takes vision. Have a vision for success, and do not lose the momentum towards your vision.

After some time, you will discover a higher and greater vision for yourself without the need to benchmark others. After two or three years of living with a clear vision of getting to the top 10% at my workplace for higher pay and faster promotion, it became impossible to lose track of the vision. Living towards a goal became a lifestyle, and I discovered higher and greater visions as I reached my daily goals. Compete it daily with the vision models, and you will eventually surpass them.

Guide to
International Business Trip

Business trips abroad became part of my life since I started managing overseas sales for HansBiomed. Flying used to excite me, and the prospect of going overseas gave me jitters. Nowadays, however, I find it difficult to leave my family for a prolonged period of time. With over 80 international exhibitions, numerous local shows, and branch meetings in the US and China, business trips have become an integral part of my corporate life.

Business trips have an element of excitement for an entry-level employee, and its easy to overlook the details of the trips. Let's review the necessary preparations.

Business trips start with booking tickets. I recommend using one or two airlines. Many airlines have a loyalty program that provides advantageous benefits when you reach a certain status. Always book a flexible ticket. Your schedule may change, so having a cheap ticket with no option for change is unfavorable. Plan the trips two to three months before the convention dates to prevent paying an excessive amount.

Use the duration of the flight to prepare for the meeting. Choose a seat diagonal from the boss with the aisle in the middle for easy communication.

Hotels must be clean, in proximity to the place of business, and have adequate amenities. Ensure that you stay in optimal condition for any business meeting. Getting a good place to relax and be comfortable is one of the top business travel tips. At breakfast, read the English version of the local newspaper. Knowing the current affairs of the local area can help to engage in small talk.

I also like to prepare a gift for the other party as a token of appreciation for making time for the meeting. This tends to ease the tension before any contract negotiation.

It may help to ask for the dress code for the meeting, but in most cases, opt for business formal. Choose the appropriate attire for any business events. Three months before the business trip, assemble a list of trip members, and delineate the purpose and goal of the trip. Review the list one month prior to the trip:

Issue / Progress/ Contract Terms / Decision maker /
Meeting agenda/ Goal/ Negotiation Terms and Limit

Elect an owner for the business trip who can manage the overall schedule and agenda. The owner is tasked with briefing the event, seminar, and convention before the trip. In our industry, registration with the given governing health agency is a crucial component of any meeting. Thus, brief the team on the registration status in the respective country. Review the following one week prior:

Email history / Contracts / Previously negotiated terms /

Any previous meeting minutes /

Goal of the meeting/ Negotiation simulation

Over breakfast, revisit all the briefed items and reiterate the purpose of the meeting with the team. Present the most up-to-date brochures and samples to the clients for a conducive discussion. A meeting on a business trip must bear fruits. Be determined to walk out of the meeting with a clear output. You represent your company when you travel for work. Don't drink excessively. Be on high alert for anything going awry.

Meeting minutes are an important tool, especially on business trips, and even more so if there is a language barrier between the two parties. Both parties should agree to the terms set forth by the meeting and sign off on the minutes. An email trace of the minutes can help to protect your party legally.

Take advantage of the airline lounge. Though some lounges only admit business class members, there are a few credit cards that offer access to airline lounges. Use the lounge to summarize the meeting and prepare for briefing before the return flight. Don't push off the paperwork and conclude the trip at the lounge.

Your first business trip may seem daunting, but if there's room in your schedule, take some time to enjoy the city. A lot of the conventions are held at vacation cities such as Miami, San Diego, Paris, Politely ask the team if you can schedule a longer stay if you'd like to take advantage of the trip. Celebrate when you have worked hard.

Workdays on business trips are twice as strenuous. We can't neglect the work of the headquarters while giving our full attention to the work at the overseas site. However, a business trip is also a favorable place to gain recognition for your work. You represent the company on the trip, and the company is making an investment by entrusting you with its responsibilities. Keep in mind what you must accomplish from the trip and be determined to walk out of any meeting with goals achieved.

Flawless Inventory

"Inventory" is an asset; it's essentially money. An open-kitchen concept restaurant must always keep the kitchen clean. In a company, such a space is a stock space in a factory. A system for organizing and maintaining warehouse storage is necessary at any company.

The most important thing in inventory management is that it must be run by the ERP editor.Note: Resource management program. No matter how small, it is good to manage ERP through a barcode. In other words, inventory must be identified in real-time at any time. The goal of inventory management is to match the computerized stock with the physical warehouse stock.

The key is to run the system so that the difference is zero. How do you do it? You should have the following criteria:

- How much should I order?
- How long does the product arrive on average after placing an order?
- What should I do to pay for my order?
- How much safety inventory should there be?
- How long does it take to check and ship the product in the loading space?

An effective system is capable of generating responds to the above questions routinely, by day, week, month, quarter, and year. Managing inventory well can save thousands of Not leaving inventory maximizes the company's profits. This can create a big problem, especially if sales executives overlook it.

- Can you prevent and act on products that are out of date?

- Can you check whether product that are out of date are left on the account?

- Are product and customer information verified when received and released?

- Is there a distinction between the ordering and ordering practitioner, the intermediate checker and the final person in charge?

Medical devices that will expire in less than six months and that are returned will have to be discarded. If your sales profit is 5%, but you are disposing of more than 10% of inventory, then your quarterly profit is -5%. It is especially discouraging to witness the expired inventory in the accounting calculation as assets.

When I started the company, I lost tens of millions of won due to a lack of experience in warehouse management. Eventually, I repaired the ERP in the warehouse for about half a year. When products are returned from the shelf of the distributor, it is a testament to failed management by the responsible employee. Its very unlikely that a company can hold employee liable for discarded inventory. An inventory manager needs to take care of the products in the company as well as going to the customer.

Smart Goal Planning

I'm a firm believer that there is a reason for everything there is a reason for your existence. Your purpose for existence may be to raise the next generation, or it may be to live day by day and enjoy what the earth provides. We are all searching for the purpose of our existence. Our life paths are determined by the means we take to reach our ultimate purpose.

However, there are only a few of us who live a purpose-driven life. We are distracted, staying focused will help you find the shortest path to your final destination.

You should ask yourself, 'What is my goal?' What is

your goal for me?

Before you do work, you have to set a goal. Whether your goal is your salary, a promotion, marriage, or sports, it is whatever you want to do and why you should do it.

You don't have to name your goal to have something that drives you. Employees whose goal is to join a company had already achieved their goals when they joined the organization. If your job was your goal, you achieved it. But now you have to have a new, more thrilling goal to make yourself move forward. Once you have started your career, set a goal to be first in the team, in the department, or in the company. The sales performance and promotion that others will envy are going to be the byproducts of achieving the goal.

You should break your goal process into years, quarters, months, and weeks, and make it easy for you to reach them easily. There must be clear excitement to achieve the goals. This is part of the training. You must take the time to design your present situation and your goals. You can do it in a quiet coffee shop. Wherever you meet yourself is good. Write down your goals first. As you write something down, you will begin to see what you want to do. It doesn't matter if it's too childish or small. Who can judge what you desire to do?

Writing them down is vastly different from thinking of them. If you have written down and displayed them where you can easily see them, you are already in the top 10% of the game.

There are very few people who can think of and organize them, and very few execute them.

Benjamin D'Railley said, "The secret to success is to have consistent goals." Take notes and inject yourself into it iteratively. Think once to write, and once again, while writing, and the beauty of repetition is given. Writing down also translates thoughts into creatures of reality and overlaps with the painful rest taken by distant ancestors in a dark cave. When we are engrossed, a new power of creation is created, and the force created entirely by us changes us slowly and develops in one direction.

Write on the paper the first thing you want to do. If you do this, you have already achieved 90% of your goal. Now, let's go to the process of creating a strategy, a plan, or how to accomplish what you need to do. If your goal is to go to Busan from Seoul, you have to choose which bus, taxi, car, train, etc. to take. The plan must be carefully planned. Unclear plans only produce unclear results. The more detailed, the more confident your results will be and the more confident you will be at moving toward your goal.

If the design process is poor, even if the building is erected, it will be awkward and insignificant, and the detailed process will be meticulous in order to reach this goal.

At this time, you will have interesting experiences, and you will feel that your goals are getting closer to reality. In other words, the process of setting goals is exciting, but if you keep writing down your goals, you may be able to do it.

The process of designing this plan now clarifies our work. On my way to the goal, my work is listed. In other words, you can do it one by one.

- Set a goal in mind
- Write down the goals on a paper
- Make plans to reach your goals
- Start on the action plan for the goal

Practice is hard. We do not brush our own teeth until we are five years old. Even easy tasks are difficult when you first put them into practice. But isn't the difference between failure and success a piece of paper? Or, whether you practiced your thoughts or not?

Every minute of the evening, you need time to look back on yourself. It doesn't matter if you play around all day. It doesn't matter if you don't get out of bed all day. But, if you want to implement a plan towards your goals, make sure you do supervision. In other words, if you sleep every night, you must think once again about whether you're going to reach the goal, or if you're going to achieve that goal today.

This one minute makes an explosive difference. If you spend the presiding time as if you were waiting for revenge each day, you will sense that the goal draws nearer with each minute. I left Daewoong Pharm after 10 years of spending 360/365 days at it when I no longer had a goal to meet every day. Even now, I write down the goals of the company, the team, and the family, and I always put them on my bedside desk as if I had an alarm clock. I think I've been able to succeed because I've always habitualized this goal-setting routine.

The goal, the specific planning and design process, and the supervision time to check the progress of my goal at least for one minute every night after implementation, along with the repetition of this cycle, are the best ways to reach the goal.

But you are bound to feel frustrated and feel hopeless. When you feel despair, seek out advice from industry leaders such as successful seniors or presidents. In other words, your initial planning and execution method may be based only on amateur strategy. Refer to those of an industry leader.

But don't make your goal too low. Be specific, but big, and set your goal higher. You have to aim for the top to land in the middle. If your aim is to be in the middle, you won't get far.

If your goal is 1st place then you will think like someone in 1st place. All outcomes are the results of your thoughts and planning. If an Olympian participates for a gold medal, he will walk away with at least a bronze medal.

Instead of always thinking about our plans and anxiously looking to the future or regretting the past, we should never forget that the present is the only reality, the only certainty; that the future almost always turns out contrary to our expectations; and that the past, too, was very different from what we suppose it to have been. But the past and the future are, on the whole, of less consequence than we think.

> *"Instead, therefore, of always thinking about our plans and anxiously looking to the future, or of giving ourselves up to regret for the past, we should never forget that the present is the only reality, the only certainty; that the future almost always turns out contrary to our expectations; that the past, too, was very different from what we suppose it to have been. But the past and the future are, on the whole, of less*

consequence than we think.

Distance, which makes objects look small to the outward eye, makes them look big to the eye of thought. The present alone is true and actual; it is the only time that possesses full reality, and our existence lies in it exclusively. Therefore, we should always be glad of it, and give it the welcome it deserves, and enjoy every hour that is bearable by its freedom from pain and annoyance with full consciousness of its value. We shall hardly be able to do this if we make a wry face over the failure of our hopes in the past or over our anxiety for the future. It is the height of folly to refuse the present hour of happiness, or wantonly to spoil it by vexation at bygones or uneasiness about what is to come. There is a time, of course, for forethought, nay, even for repentance, but when it is over, let us think of what has past as something to which we have said farewell to; of necessity subduing our hearts."

- from Essay of Schopenhauer

Predicting Results
with Closing

There are many forms of closing, such as daily closing, weekly closing, monthly closing, quarterly closing, semi-annual closing, and annual closing. In any company, sales-related departments have closings and deadlines. Therefore, the deadline for interim checks is a very important step toward the goal. A daily deadline and a weekly deadline will, of course, lead to the goal of management. Wouldn't it be possible to meet your goals by making sure you cross the BEP breakeven?

Can you play baseball or soccer without knowing how many victories your team will need to go to the finals? Or, what the difference between the points is and how much time is available?

In other words, routine closings are markers for ensuring that you are in route to achieve the deadline and goals. That is why weekly work or daily reporting is important. Repetitive tasks of reporting will get easier the more you practice. These reports guide performances.

The daily, weekly, monthly, or quarterly deadlines, etc., however, are not always good. For example, if you sell 100 bowls of rice, and if there is a restaurant with a monthly balance, then shouldn't it be 50 bowls on the 15th day? Even if you set a higher target, you still have to sell 60 bowls. What if you sell only 30 bowls? The process of confirming this is the deadline.

All employees should analyze what they have or have not done at their respective position. All members of the department should have the same goal and each level or employees should organize an agenda of what can be done to achieve the goal.

After answering the above questions, calculate the GAP with the target. Also, identify new accounts as well as accounts whose sales have fallen. What is the BEP for an account? Have you surpassed the BEP? If not, what was the issue? What short term incentive was offered to temporary increase sales?

This is to see if there is anything that can be done, whether to improve the communication conduit, or to hire a specialist in this field.

If you have only three employees who don't have a deadline, a team leader who doesn't have a deadline, and three department managers who don't have a deadline, your goal will be lost.

I advise you to not become preoccupied with the target at first. It's essential that you develop the basic skills that will ultimately help you reach the goal.

When to Search for
a New Job

I have experienced leaving a position for a new job, starting a company, and managing a company as an executive. But like many others, I once had to make the hard decision of leaving a company.

There is always a beginning and an end. Where you start your career is the most important decision. Most people stay in the department that they started out in. If you start out in sales, you transition to another sales position, and marketing to marketing. The first task and your first boss will greatly influence your first transition. We move for many reasons, such as for salaries, benefits, promotions, conflicts with our bosses, and career goals.

However, there are a few important questions you must first ask yourself. As long as you work with people, there will always be similar issues.

First, discern if you are unhappy with the work, or if you are discontent with the people you work with. If you are unhappy with the work, then you have to asses if you have fallen into a slump and reassess your roles and responsibilities. Seek a superior's opinion. It may be that you are in a slump because you do not see rapid results. If you are discontent with your colleagues, evaluate whether changes can be made. Can you transition to a different team? Or, is there any imminent restructuring.

Second, assess your readiness for a move. Economic matters are very important. Don't quit your company on a whim. Don't quit because you want to go on a soul-searching journey; you will come back to the same problems of reality.

In fact, you need to regain middle-ground and restore your physical and mental state. Continue to take night-shift breaks for both the mind and the body, minimize overtime, and invest your all only during the working hours. Exercising and continued learning may not change anything but are an essential means to manage your emotional and physical health.

I often tell my employees, "I exercise, study, and sleep early so that I can continue working and enjoy life to the fullest." Investing in yourself rather than binging on extreme pleasures such as over-eating and drinking is the key to stress management. Any activity that harms the body puts more stress in your life.

'*The Life Class*', by Elisabeth Kubler-Ross and David Kessler, states:

"*Work and play do not have to be completely separate activities. Finding pleasure in what you do is desirable. Finding joy in everyday things can help you live your day and live your life.”*

Why don't you think of making your company a playground, for exercising and playing?

Anyway, the bottom line is to check out if you are ready to leave the company and see if you can do anything in the new place that you can't do in the old one. If the answer is YES, consider moving.

Your time to move to a new company may come sooner than expected. I am not opposed to turnover. You have to find out where your mental and physical values fit.

If you think you should turn away, try to share your concerns and anxieties with your team leader and business manager with the utmost courtesy. If you still find it difficult to change your mind, you should communicate at least one month in advance and go your way. Sometimes, there is an answer.

At this time, colleagues around you lack experience, so please consult with your company's role model. Isn't it necessary to take the enemy with me? If you think about it, it's a thankful place for me to study.

If you change your job too often, the letters of recommendation may not be as good, and you will have less work and less help. Discuss your thoughts with others around you and move on if you have a decision. It is distressing to lose talented employees. However I remain hopeful about their professional growth and the positive impact they will have on the industry.

Daily Resolution
for a Joyful Day

If you can have everything, will you be happy?

You may still feel groggy when you wake up in the morning. You may lose the determination and motivation you had when you first started working and live for the weekends and holidays.

Are you experiencing a slump? Is it your coworkers? Your boss? Or is it a lack of recognition for your work? We all have a desire to perform and succeed. I've given my resignation multiple times, so I can sympathize with the employee's internal struggles.

Where can we find happiness? I thought I would be happy when I got a job, I would be happy when I got married, I would be happy when I had a pretty baby, I would be happy when I bought a house. Where is the bluebird?

You spend most of your time at work. If you don't count the hours that you are asleep, most of your life's waking moments are spent at the workplace. If this workplace becomes a hell for you, then you are doomed to a life of misery. So then how can we find happiness at work?

First, you must learn to be optimistic. There are always pessimists at work who cannot stop complaining. Avoid such people at all costs. Start by filtering out people who do not add value to your life. There is a biblical phrase that teaches, "do not walk in the counsel of the wicked or stand in the way of the sinners or sin in the seat of the mockers."

Have you ever met a successful pessimist? Optimism improves those around you, but pessimism drags them down. Optimism inspires people to great heights. Pessimism deflates people to new lows. Avoid those who spend the day slandering others in the workplace.

Second, don't hesitate to volunteer your resources. Always jump in to grab opportunities but ask for help from others. Don't wait for work to be passed down to you; take the initiative. The company is a place to obtain experience. Those with the most experience in the shortest amount of time will rise faster and farther on the corporate ladder. That is, a person who works a lot and has more experience is promoted often. It's simple logic. There is no promotion if you do less work. If you are working, you may be buried in the job, but if you are a proxy, you can tell if you need more people.

Third, always plan. Plan your work, your goals, your vacations. The schedule should be tightly packed. You should plan to rest. Exercise plans should be set, as well as when to meet up with friends.

In particular, there should be rest, play, and vacation planning. If you have a plan, you will move forward. You are ready to work when you are ready. Have daily, weekly, monthly, quarterly, and annual plans. Planning will help you get in balance. Life is about how well you juggle different aspects of your tasks.

Strive to maintain a balance in all aspects of work and life. Keep a balance between work and health. Do not lose your hobby by being engrossed with work.

We reevaluate and plan life and work in order to obtain the balance. Finding a happy medium will bring you joy in all circumstances.

Part 2

Relationship
Strategy

Different Leaders

In an ideal world, we would have managers who display exceptional leadership, have decision-making capabilities, and are knowledgeable. Unfortunately, that is not always the case. You may have experienced a manager who isn't very competent and shows a lack of good character.

If you observe your boss for a few days, you will be able to make a judgment on his abilities. you don't have to be a baseball fan to tell when a player is good. Similarly, you do not have to be a manager to comprehend the abilities of your boss. What can you make out of the situation? Can you learn from a person with minimal merit?

There is an old proverb, "Of evil manners spring good laws." You can use such circumstances for your benefit. If your boss is overly competent, your work is not likely to receive any recognition, but when a superior displays a lack of competency, then you will outshine him.

The leadership of the company will notice the quality of the work that you produce. Anticipate the tasks that your manager expects and make some leadership decisions on your own.

Adversity is the greatest teacher. Every hardship and failure has its benefits. When you are faced with a problematic task, reach out to other departments to collaborate on finding the best solution. In the midst of maneuvering through hurdles, you will gain the experience and skill set that will help you grow in your career.

Our first jobs, first projects, and first bosses of our

professional careers are crucial. Your first job will make you better for your second, third, and fourth jobs in the next decade and more. It is truly a blessing to work under a respectable boss. You will come across a wide spectrum of management. It's the bosses who are going to influence what you become, who is going to guide you into opportunity. It's the boss who has the power to make you miserable or thrilled.

It is surprisingly beneficial for our productivity to work under lazy managers. If you provide punctual and adequate feedback to the boss, your boss will entrust you with more work and ultimately add to your skillset. It's hard to grow when you're being micromanaged. It is extremely frustrating to work with a boss who doesn't trust you and only looks out for their own interests.

Working under an overly diligent manager can also be challenging. The boss may delegate too much tasks or reject your enthusiastic ideas. Try to see their hands-on approach as an opportunity for mentorship. Your new boss may be trying to find ways to help, so be more receptive.

How do you describe your ideal boss? In the corporate world, where the main objective of the relationship is business, it is difficult to develop deeper relationships with bosses and colleagues. An ideal boss understands your skills and capabilities but also understands your individual goals and objectives-both in your career and in your personal life.

An ideal leader is kind, understanding, encouraging, and constructive. Corporations invest in growing such leaders because they understand that one of the key factors in job happiness or unhappiness is our relationship with our boss. A good boss can make a bad job tolerable or even enjoyable, while a bad boss can turn an otherwise gratifying occupation into a miserable one.

A good boss should understand the goals and objectives of the company as well as where you want to go with your career. Ideally, your boss will instruct you to move in right direction that can complement both the companies' and individual desires. He will also guide you to recognize the skills that you'll need and assign tasks where you can develop such skills. You may also learn through observing how your boss handles tasks.

The worst boss is someone who is hands-off, is not specific regarding expectations for performance, and leaves you to face the problem alone.

If your boss doesn't possess leadership skills, look around you for managers who do. Politely ask them to guide and mentor you to perform better. Career planning in business is usually associated with performance reviews. A useful performance review should happen whenever it's appropriate.

I often approach my tennis club mates with the same

attitude. I ask for opinions on my performance and ask them for tips. It's hard to imagine anyone turning away such a polite request. It may be a bit uncomfortable and cool at first to approach others, but they may appreciate that your acknowledge their foresight. It is hard to find seniors who turn away someone asking for help.

When you approach your boss, be polite and sincere yet be direct in your question. Let him know your struggle and your desire to do better. The more experienced members have walked through the same path you you. They too know the pressure of deadline and hurdles of projects. Have an honest conversation with your struggles with your boss and he will suggest a solution.

It is not only the deadline that is important. Routinely report to the management on the progress so that they have a clear understanding of your work, and monitor the direction as well.

If your boss is making you miserable at work and you can't learn anything from him, rely on the company for human resource actions. A reliable company will identify such an inadequate leader. If your company has failed to do so, then you may need to consider leaving the company.

Leadership Qualities

Do you ever wonder why a CEO gets paid more? Higher pay in real terms means higher risk. If there is higher risk that comes with the job, then the company will naturally pay more competitively. Higher risk means higher pay, and lower risk means lower pay. When employees, supervisors, deputy managers, and managers do not perform and cause loss, the company cannot hold them liable. There is practically no personal damage.

The two quintessential attitudes of a leader are one, resourcefulness and two, role model mentality. Outcomes are built on this. A manager must be someone who employees respect and follow.

Being resourceful means knowing exactly what the purpose of the work is, how to achieve the result, and telling the employees the right direction. One has to comprehend the nature of work in order to plan how to carry out a task.

Many companies conduct meetings without a clear explanation for the reason. Most attendees are, therefore, oblivious to what the meeting can accomplish. The manager must organize other departments, analyze different business areas, acquire new knowledge, and understand a lot of information going on in the industry, as well as share it with team members.

At a young age, I became a general manager and business manager. For the first ten years of my career I worked 350 days out of 365 days a Perhaps a successful person works just as much, if not more. As a young kid, I wasn't the brightest. When I became an adult, I knew that I had to work harder than anyone else to get to the

top. This mentality helped me get to where I am faster.

There is a saying that to make a company profitable, get rid of desks. Even now, I routinely visit all our customers. It's often extremely tiring to carry out these visits along with desk work. However, maintaining relationships with the customers is a priority.

Do they have any complaints? Is our marketing effective? What is the competitor up to? The quickest way to find out is to stay in the field. In this way, you can be the first to know what issues your employees are having these days and can solve them quickly. The employee does not talk to the company right away, so I have to take care of it.

There is a reason why team leaders receive allowance. Whatever it is, that era is over. The boss, the team leader, is one of the owners of the company and should be the primary role model for new employees and subordinates.

Company Event
with Uppers Management

In our hierarchical culture, spending time with the boss after a long working day then at a company dinner is distressing., In fact, the boss and executives are always curious. High-level bosses, such as executives, want to listen to the people company dinner is an opportunity to see the company's strategy, policies, and systems in place. Bosses and executives always like to spend time with new or smart employees.

How should we prepare for these difficult times? If you are anxious, remember the following four things:

- What are you working on now? and what are your goals?

- Are things going as planned?
- Why and why not?
- What can your company do to help you achieve that goal?

Be prepared to answer these questions. In fact, our work revolves around the four questions.

The above questions have to be sorted out in order to do the actual work, but most do not think about the specific purposes, goals, and plans of my work as the top four item. An employee who can answer the four questions effortlessly without an intention to flaunt is reliable. Management will appreciate such an employee.

You may become subjected to jealousy by others if your boss recognizes you over the others. However, jealousy is ever present and you shouldn't let it deter you from standing out There is a professor I know who writes a lot of papers and broadcasts to a lot of people around him, so many people can be jealous. So I asked how to solve this, and the answer is a masterpiece.

> *"You shouldn't be a little better than others, and you should be very good at making a big difference. Then at some point, jealousy gradually begins to turn into respect for the results and results of my work."*

Living with goals and goals in mind like numbers 1-4 is how people with successful habits become respected executives.

During a company dinner, a senior manager sometimes opens the floor for employees to give their opinion. The hour can become very uncomfortable. If no one speaks, the air of silence gets suppressing, and if one does speak too freely the tension in the room rises.

The most important thing to watch out for is negative thoughts and tone. Negative thoughts and speech are

highly contagious, making it the number one alert for team leaders and presidents. When you are in a negative or bad mood at work, you should ask yourself why and avoid drinking as much as possible. If you have a hard conversation, it's best to go to your boss 24 hours later and be as polite as possible.

If you ask a question, rather than asking your boss or executives about the company's policies and the content of the system, you may want to ask about the intent and why they were implementing the system and policies. If you ask about intentions, your boss can tell you in more detail, It's also a good idea to ask why it was necessary and implemented for the content of the company's usual interest. Employees should also be interested the company's policies and systems. If all members of a company shared the same background knowledge on policy, operations, and vision, imagine how much easier it would be to collaborate amongst them.

Conflict Resolution

Conflicts with colleagues and supervisors are inevitable in the workplace. Conflict is natural with your coworkers, When conflicts arise, team leaders may step in to mediate the situations but they are not usually successful. This is because most of the team leaders were recognized for their performance not their inter-personal skills. Even without a team leader and no mediator, we have to solve the case. To solve the problem, it is necessary to analyze the problem as follows.

- What is the cause of the conflict?
- What are the possible solutions?

- Will I do the same if I'm on the opposite side?
- Is the decision for the team rather than myself, or for the company rather than the team?
- Have I ever sought advice from a third party who can view the problem objectively?

First, it is always preferred to clarify the cause. If you fight without knowing what the problem is, you fight without a reason. Also, the emotional response to these things will amplify the problem. In most problematic situations, you are prone to can get angry at someone you don't like. You may come off as too emotional if you don't take a logical approach.

Second, if the cause of the problem has been clarified, a solution must be devised and implemented immediately. You may consider different communication conduit to approach the conflict; through a boss, directly, or wait for the situation to die down.

Email is easy to misunderstand. In particular, text messages sent immediately in anger are likely to lack reason, so please do not send them. It takes courage to overcome discomfort. During a conflict, attitude and tone of the voice can exacerbate the situation. Ninety percent of time, people fight more about the meaning of the words used, be polite and modest when approaching any situation.

The third and fourth point is to consider others 'perspectives'. Most of the time if you look at it objectively, other parties view seem reasonable. It's not about accepting opinions, but thinking about them from their point of view. Ultimately, the conflict should lead to a decision to benefit the interest of the company and the organization.

Fifth, it may be helpful to seek mediation or advice from those who can see the problem objectively. Thus, if you're familiar with people in other departments, ask for their advice. When I work, I strive to see the bigger picture and co-work with other teams. When people have a problem, listening to the opinions of several people will clear up their thoughts. Do not rely heavily on others to provide a solution because they may not be qualified or knowledgeable enough to advise you. Therefore have a low expectation when seeking advices.

Conflicts among colleagues are ubiquitous at all companies. If these conflicts are left unresolved and snowball they can lend to bigger problems. Problems can cause misunderstandings, and a series of misunderstandings can cause irreparable anger or team division.

Growing through Interaction

Societal view tells us that working at a large corporation is desirable. Almost everyone desires a high salary and a stable job, but the reality is that the outcome of professional career at a large corporation isn't always favorable. Working at mega corporation has its drawbacks. For one your employment is not secured after certain position. You also become slaved to the system and lose autonomy.

Large companies have a well-organized system, so naturally, a company can draw a short-term plan and a long-term, systematic business structure. In addition, since the roles and divisions of personnel, finance, marketing, and sales are clearly distinguished, it is possible to avoid problems caused by ambiguity.

Upsides of small business are direct access to upper management and quicker promotions. It's hard to say that working at one is better than other because there are no right answer. Sometimes, It is what you make of it.

Luck plays a role at work. Even if you join a company you want, you may not get assigned to the department you want. Build a list of criteria to help you decide where to start off your career. I would set the criteria for choosing a job as follows.

- Is your business group a growing business group?
- Is what you are pursuing relevant to the contemporary?
- Do you think your beliefs and management philosophy align?
- Do you believe that your company works according to your business philosophy?
- Can I learn and grow here?

Everyone must find his or her own path.

Not everyone will become a CEO. Sufficient time and experience are necessary for you to discover the path fulfill your purpose in life. In fact, the size of the company may matter, but the growth depends on who you've worked with and what your boss has learned. Indeed, I was fortunate to learn about HansBiomed and its breakthrough product development. I was able to envision my future with the company. Previous to HansBiomed, I received guidance from the chairman Yun of Daewoong on how to grow professionally. In other words, who I met is the foundation of my growth. As I mentioned before in smaller business you are in contact with upper managements. Their advices may be more valuable than a fancy name on your resume.

People grow according to who they meet. Pursue a reputable role model. That can be more helpful than moving to a different company. Whether you're a small business or a large company, look around, and find a mentor.

Key
to Hiring

HansBiomed's human resource pool has widened significantly since I became the CEO. The company's internal value is important, but application pool has increased drastically since we moved to the current building To a new recruit exterior building of the company and reputation of the management system are just important factors in choosing a career. However, Just as we can't make a judgment about a restaurant based on one menu, you should also consider atmosphere, service, growth, other factors in choosing a company.

I look for a genuine personality when hiring, and so did many companies that I've worked with, An ideal person is genuine, considerate of others and confident.

As Stephen Covey said in The Seven Habits of Effective People, the root of the tree determines the value of the tree. The root signifies the character of a person and the rest of the leave represents external personality. What if there are troublemakers who have skills and abilities but create negative and discords among colleagues. For teamwork and organization, it is better to have a person with noble character that withstands the harshest circumstance than a high performing trouble maker. A troublemaker who cannot cohabit is an envoy.

The next condition is the ability of the individual. If you set a measure to assess ability, you can think of it as intellectual ability, or a learning ability, For those who are always exercising, learning a new sport comes easy. If they are taught, they will soon be able to follow. For example, if you give a thesis to an avid reader they will be able to summarize the material and report back to you on the content of the paper. The body and mind do not experience difficulties when they are trained to do what they normally have done. Thus, we must be prepared to learn and hone the ability to learn.

Both GPA and TOEIC test scores can be earned with constant effort, so high scores suggest that the candidate was studious and persistent, Studying is not just a matter of will but takes persistent practice. You may have experienced making a New Year's resolution to exercise then failing to stay on track after just few weeks. It takes takes will power and strong discipline to turn resolution into a lifestyle. There are a few questions I always ask to assess their fit with the company:

- Why should we hire you? (Entry and mid-level)
- Why are you looking to move? (Mid-level)

The candidates should persuade interviewers through their values and motivations. New-hires who have passed through to the end of the assessment now face the second evaluation: internship. During the internship/

probation period, company evaluates other qualifications that have not been brought to light during a two- to three-hour interview. For at least three to six months, there is a probation period to get to know each other and make sure you can work with the team. Human resources team is responsible for smooth transition for the new hire. His or her experience at the new company heavily depends on the team and the team leader. During the three-to six-month probationary period, team leaders discuss with their HR team what they will evaluate.

- Attitude (positive, active, commute time, conversation methods, business manners compliance)
- Performance (learning skills and passion for work during internships)

Through this objective data, we choose to hire, nurture, and work with the idea of 'personality is everything.'

The job of the boss, officer, and leader is to hire the right people, to teach and nurture them to become the next leaders.

Responsibilities of New Manager

Often, when a high performing employee becomes a manager, he or she struggles to adapt to the new position. Motivation alone is not enough to fulfill the role since team leaders are not likely to The new manager's motivation alone is not enough to fulfill the role since the team members will not readily concede to his or her direction. In the overall leadership pipeline, the first level manager faces the most significant challenge. Not only do you have to evaluate yourself as an employee, but also as a team leader; often the new managers oversee team of people who are still in the learning phase.

In fact, the primary stress that these team leaders have is the pain of having employees below, not from seniors. Occasionally, the subsidiary's immaturity makes sense, but if they lack passion for performance, it's difficult to tolerate them.

If so, what should the team leader do with his/her entry, assistant manager level employees? Should you listen to them first? The first thing to do is to engage in coaching. Coaching is the process of assisting capable employees if they are currently wandering and deviating from the goal. But if an employee with less than a year of work does not welcome your input or have apprehension about his or her work, then the leader should review the employee's comprehension of the system.

It is the team leader's role first to explain the company, team and personal goals to the new employees, discuss what strategies and methods needed to achieve them, and fully understand and sympathize with them.

Elucidate the purpose of the work, goals and how to accomplish them.

If you neglect such time, the team may struggle to stay on track. Trying to go a little faster is counterproductive. That's why team leaders should check their weekly reports on Mondays or Fridays to see if goals, directions, and goals are working. Team members are not yet skilled at work. The team leader should inform the employees about the four quadrants:

- Important and urgent work
- Not important but urgent
- Not urgent but important
- Neither important nor urgent

When you fail to prioritize and sort work into different categories, you find that you are working long hours without much result. The tasks that fall under the first category must be completed first. However, how much you can accomplish depends on how faithfully you have been working on the third category. Working through the third category will decrease the tasks that fall under urgent work, and you will see an increase in productivity, as well as performance. On the other hand, you must prevent the items in the second list from increasing. An employee may make the mistake of thinking that he or she is doing important work because it is urgent, but he or she is wasting time on unimportant matters.

Calls, fax, or emails are not important tasks; we often describe them as "work," but they never help achieve the goal. Therefore, the team leader should teach the team to value the three most important tasks.

The team leader is not the person who does the job but the person who produces the results by distributing work. It's no surprise that many new team leaders think of themselves as good, productive, and competent people. However, they should always bear in mind the stationary limb. They need to take good care of the people below them.

In particular, if high performers are promoted early and become team leaders, reflect to when they first joined as a new employee. Encourage the team to work according to these categories for better workflow. There may be members of the team who lack skills and abilities, but they learn, and your ability as a leader will determine how long the learning will take. A great leader leads the team to become the best version that each member can be.

Kevin Cashman wrote the following in his book '*Leadership from Inside Out*':

> "*One of the most important qualities a leader must have is openness—openness to new market possibilities, openness to new learning and strategies, openness to human relationships, openness to new ways of doing business, and openness to stimulating*

people to pursue possibilities."

A leader of the team does not have possession over the team. New and immature leaders build walls and close off their team from other teams. They also make the mistake of hoarding the work stunting the growth of the team. When a team member's productivity increase, your skill as a manager also increases and will lighten your workload. As leaders we have the duty to raise next generation of leaders.

Encourage the members to seek advices from experts of the respective field and to expand their knowledge through seminars, and books. Employees will thrive under a climate emboldens their growth. Kwang-Won Seo writes in '*Living as a President*' as follows:

"A leader must posses composure and compassion."

Standing at the extreme is burdensome. Therefore, it is necessary to distinguish between the task.

Danger of
Blind Trust

Do you believe in the company? What do you believe? Do we believe in seeing? Or is seeing believing? On the contrary, when we are deceived, what deceived you?, Was did your expectation deceive you?

We need to understand what it means to trust work, company and people. When a company hires employees, the company believes in the employees first and entrusts them to carry out their parts. If you go to the bank as a company president you will require tremendous collateral but in the case of employees, the company believes in them. A problem arises when company does not fulfill the promised offers and with hold salaries, benefits. Employees begin to doubt the company. At times such promises fall through due to loss in profit or financial crises but there are very few employees who will sympathize with the situation. On the other hand, when an employee does not perform, the company distrusts the employee.

This creates distrust between the company, team leader, and team members. And as negative convictions continue to accumulate, hostility intensifies and employees begin to consider leaving the company. What really went wrong?

What standard should you have when evaluating yourself? Expect 120%; Have a critical and strict standard for yourself. In other words, there is 40% gap between expectation for others versus yourself. This is the buffer. When there is enough buffer, you will feel less likely to feel angry or betrayed. That is, you can reduce your desire for the company, for work, for your team leader. This will gradually bring happinessand leisure And because you are strict with yourself, tolerant of others, you will be humble about your accomplishments and appreciating of others performance.

Are there any negative consequences of such behavior? The boss and the executive have looked at people for 20 to 30 years. Do you think you can't distinguish between a person who evaluates his own as 120 and a person who evaluates as 80, and vice versa? People who are promoted are often the humble and considerate ones, not the best performing ones We live in culture that esteems congeniality, cooperation, and communication.

A team leader came by saying he was deceived by an employee. Employees were quitting and preparing to go to another company, and he was so stressed that the takeover would happen in a week, despite the policy requiring a month of advance notice. The staff said that they had a drink a week ago and shrugged off a problem together.

I responded as follows: First of all, you expected too much. Employees have the freedom to quit as they wish. Don't be bothered about a staff leaving; people live together for decades and break up. There are things 100 times depressing than an employee leaving. Second, if you have done weekly reports, monthly reports, on-site checks every week, then you should know your account relationships, and know more about your customers than your employees. What's your concern? why does it trouble you so much that a employee is leaving? Perhaps you have been relying on the employee too much and worried about the new workload.

You should trust the data obtained by checking the customer's satisfaction, visit status, new business situation, and change of discontinued customers. If you had been aware of the trend in the data of your employee, you would have predicted his departure from the company.

People often believe something vague. They hold on to a vague idea that lamentable events will not occur to them. The idea is not a belief but actually a superstition. Faith is a combination of thorough preparation and experiences.

Expecting 100% from others is the main source of a problem. Always expect 80% from others and accept and appreciate work produced by them.

Trust needs to be nurtured and developed. You can only ask, "Do you trust me?" if your relationship has deepened over time.

Business Etiquette

Some people are hated despite their hard work, and some gain favor despite the lack of effort. Spain's leading philosopher, Balthazar Grassian, said in his book, 'The Most Selfish Advice in the World':

> "The easiest way to gain a lot with little effort is by being courteous."

Once you get started, it's important to conserve your image as a polite person.

There was an incident that I vividly remember to this day. Ten years ago, when I was in sales, I visited a doctor at his clinic. We chatted for a while, and then I got up to leave. His facial expression gave away that something was wrong, so I sat back down.

I asked, "did I do something wrong?" He responded with an unexpected answer. "I'm going to give you advice because I see your potential to succeed. When you greet people, do it with sincerity, and take time to show respect. "That day, I returned home and, in front of a mirror, replayed how I greeted him earlier. I saw that I was, in fact, just nodding my head. I felt greatly embarrassed and ashamed. Since that incident, I have taken a full two seconds to greet others. It is my way of showing respect and reminding myself to stay humble.

I became interested in business manners from that time-how to wear clothes, how to laugh, how to prepare documents, and how to speak politely.

- Give heartfelt greetings to everyone involved, even those around you.
- Remember the names and birthdays of employees.

- Implement commitments promptly (prompt feedback on progress and results).

- Always arrive 20 minutes before your appointment.

- Seek understanding at least 30 minutes to 1 hour before your appointment.

- Do not make unreasonable promises from the beginning.

- Avoid excessive commitments when drinking.

- Complete tasks that involve others first

- Speak in honorific to new employees

- Be good to the superiors and not just to the others

- Always ask for consent before holding a company dinner

On the road, blinking the high beam twice is a gesture of apology. These polite gestures exist in sales and are essential in conducting business. Being polite never hurts. Courtesy includes greetings, appointments, actions, and manners. When you make these principles, you are resilient to them, and the relationship will remain pleasant. If you can create and enjoy a humble and enjoyable relationship yourself, your company life will soon become more natural. 'Work and Life Balance.' is popular. It is not difficult to match the coined word "Waraval," which means work-life balance. When a company naturally finds pleasure in a relationship, it gets by itself. For him, a good attitude is needed, which is humility. This good habit goes a lifetime.

How can we cultivate this courtesy and humility, the most important of interpersonal relationships? Humility is not pretending to be humble.

Company Culture and Values

The staff can't always be of like mind. There are situations where a qualified employee suddenly quits, and sometimes the enthusiasm of a passionate employee dies down. They even betray you.

Team leaders should be concerned about their role at such moments. Uphold the value and philosophy of the company, team and yourself through the difficult times. As a manager, you must have the duty to convey company's vision and values to the employees and assist them in adapting it to their own.

Shared organizational values must be continuously

highlighted in every corner of the company by departments and even by interns and part-time students. The values should apply to all personnel and ubiquitous all operations. Companies with strong core values will endure hardships and construct robust infrastructure. For instance, if the core philosophy is "learning new knowledge," we should take time to discuss and share how to achieve goals during weekly and monthly meetings.

As such, the corporate must continuously encourage and educate the values to the employees. Employees who accept these values and practice them are subjected to fair performance evaluation. Even if there are one or two unreasonable team leaders and business managers, the results should be reasonable to everyone.

Next, the goals must be shared, and the reasons for achieving these goals should be clear. Like a compass, a leader must determine the direction of the organization the rest of the team why the path is essential.

The team loses the trajectory in the absence of discussion about the share target. When you can no longer find the desire to work, ask yourself or your colleagues the if there is an intention and a reason to attain the goal. The company has many jobs. You do things without specific goals and justifications, but you do it for work, not for achieving your goals. Such work cannot lead to accomplishment. If you eradicate scores for soccer or basketball, for what would the players play? When an organization presents a goal and discusses how to win the game, it motivates the members to achieve that target.

The outlook of employees will begin to change with each discussion. Not all will display such evolution but if they display even 30% of change in perspective, they have the potential to be a leader. However, I do not think that a 30% chance of changing perspectives is enough to be qualified as a team leader.

However, at times due to favorable market condition you obtain results without a clear target. Such results are not a testament to your ability. What you do is not your own ability. Of course, there are freebies and luck in life. Don't overestimate yourself because of these accidental results.

Making goals specific and feasible is critical to organizational management.Organizations are actively moving when they run with clear goals.

Once the corporate values and goals are established, team leaders and managers must coordinate collaborating in shaping the strategy to work effectively with the departments involved. Thus, with company-wide The better organized a corporation, the more time it spends on 'preparing work' by devising strategies to achieve the objectives. The process may feel prolonged but the strategies and objectives produced will be upstanding. Don't be afraid to invest a lot of time.

The philosophy and quantitative goal setting mentioned above are the keys to moving an organization. Additionally, a manager should monitor the sites routinely to confirm that the objectives are implemented. In other words, increase communication with the sites. Performance is proportional to the time spend with the customers. As you continue to meet and talk with your customers, you will see why it's important to meet them at the team leader level.

The boss and executives must always keep their ears open to the accounts they manage. The organization's philosophical value must be internalized to ensure that team, and individual goals are implemented to the field.

When an employee cannot achieve his target, first assess his knowledge of the strategy. How do you solve a problem without knowing the cause? Instead of reprimanding the staff, the team leader must ask oneself and thinks about how to supervise him at this eye level. An employee may not know why and what to do. To check the success of the planned strategy, the team leader conducts a complete survey of 30% personal relations, 30% of neutral relationships, and 30% of places that have no relationship. The outcome of the survey is a forecast of what the staff should prepare for.

Leading an organization is not as easy as it sounds. The team leader should treat the staff with the warmest heart of the team, teaching and assisting young novices to survive in this difficult society. It's not easy, but don't forget that raising people is one of the team's most important roles. After all, the best way to learn is by teaching.

Part 3

Marketing and Sales Strategy

First Role of
Marketing Team

I started my career in marketing in 2003. The world of marketing continues to expand, and with the recent developments in the marketing field, it continues to be more challenging. Several marketing team employees complain about the lack of clarity with their roles. They often play the role of sales assistants, operations personnel, and event coordinators. In a mid-size company, especially, marketing is an area that requires extensive resources and investment.

The primary goal of inbound marketing is to create a marketing platform to accentuate the features of the product and understand the psychology of the customers' needs.

The process of accentuating the features involves brochures, symposiums, advertisements, seminars, and more. Many medical device companies overlook the importance of a strong marketing team and focus on attending large congresses and creating medical brochures. Someone who was involved in such activities is unlikely to have substantial knowledge and experience in marketing. A good marketer has a clear understanding of the needs of the customers and what features of the product can create a solution for them.

We are regularly exposed to marketing and advertisements for brands. Branding makes the customers believe that in purchasing luxury cars like BMW, Mercedes and Maserati, they are buying the image of success. How do these companies succeed in creating a branding image that sets them apart from the competitors? Yong Mi Moon discusses how to create an effective branding strategy in her book 'Different'

"Marketers must pay close attention to brand ambassadors. In-N-Out Burger is not a favorite for everyone but has a following of loyal customers. In the restaurant industry, obtaining such avid followers who are passionate about the brand is an impressive accomplishment.

A marking PM is someone who continues the conversation with these customers and has an insight into what features engage the customers."

BellaGel is a breast implant that Hans offers. Although BellaGel is a remarkable product, it needs to compete with implants from giant companies. Allegan's yearly revenue is close to 20 billion USD, and J&J's is 100 billion USD. With revenues less than 1 million USD, all the odds were stacked up against BNS when it entered into the implant market. I sought out guidance from the most renowned doctors of Korea: Dr. Seul, the CEO of JW Plastic Surgery, Dr. Yoon, the CEO of MeGo Plastic Surgery, Dr. Choi, the CEO of Grace Plastic Surgery., Professor Shim of Soon Chun Hyang

University, Professor Heo from Seoul University Bundang campus. They advised me on advantageous features of these implants and helped to construct the brand image for BellaGel: "Implant designed for Asians, BellaGel." Through marketing conversation, we discovered the need for implants designed to best fit Asian women, who, on average, are smaller in chest size than Caucasians. We emerged into the market with 12% of the market share. When BellaGel Smooth Fine was introduced featuring enhanced safety and surface, the market share rose to 23%. In the 13 years since the introduction of implants in Korea, BNS is the first company to have the most market share and get ahead of the two mega-companies.

We focused more on engaging customers, finding the need of the customers, and marketing the differentiating features of our brand. Marketing is essentially a conversation between a business and its customers.

< Law of Lanchester Hunei >

7% recognizable

11% participation

15% superior presence

26% Distinction

31% distinctive dominance

42% market leader (controls the market)

74% monopoly (occupies the monopoly position)

Customer enthusiasts don't just know our products.

Let's check. The above list is a quantified way to reasonably assess your activity. How much do you know about your competitors and their presence in the market? What do the customers prefer? The next is, "I am fully concerned about the impact of the market."

To ask the question, where is my position in the market? And accordingly, do you fix it? Do you have a competitor?

Second Role of
Marketing Team

The marketing team is one of the departments that work behind the scenes. Many marketing team members complain that they are gaining experience but not obtaining new skills. Then what is the role of the marketing team? Furthermore, there is less freedom in marketing medical devices due to stringent medical laws that limit the scope of marketing activities.

However, I still think that I should continue to carve the way. Sales make the way, but planning the road is the job of marketing.

People who are involved in marketing are called marketers. Marketers from labs work in research, and marketers from sales focus on the selling point for marketing, and will often reflect their background knowledge. "We're discovering product features and differentiating them from other products, and if we don't find one, we can create it and effectively communicate it to our customers, increasing our market share, sales, and profits." This is the role of the marketer.

Product is also the most crucial portion of marketing. If the "Product" is not good, it would be unwise to spend a lot of money on marketing. Customers are many times smarter than we think, so even if they buy a product due to the effective marketing, they are not likely to repurchase the product if they are unsatisfied with their purchases. In other words, even a successful marketing product will see re-purchases only when the product has notable features and differentiation. Then, how do you successfully market 'difference'?

First, marketers should inquire with at least ten experts for their opinion on the products. As I have always said, consult with experts whom you have a good relationship with, a neutral relationship with, or no association in 3:3:3 ratio. It is a blessing to meet an expert who is both kind and informative. Record and consider their opinions in creating a marketing platform.

Next, organize the collected data. In particular, medical devices are different from medicines, and the results may differ depending on the doctor's skill, training, and the surgery or procedure. You can market how many cases were carried out at various hospitals and, how many accumulated results you have.

At the end of this stage, marketers and sales managers meet to document the cases. If more than 30~40% of customers understand the marketing strategy and agree on the characteristics and results of the product, then the marketing plan is successful. The director and PM should meet to not only talk about the product but also summarize the attributes of the products by gathering a consensus from experts in the field.

In the case of MINT, an absorbable face lifting suture, we witnessed explosive sales growth when experts' experience and opinion became well-known. It is now our best selling product exporting to about 70 countries. We also created a "Mint Expert Meeting(M.E.M.)" where doctors from all over the world, including the US and Brazil, gathered to share more cases and contents. They are encouraged by the success of surgical techniques and materials by the power of collective knowledge. A group worked on organizing a strategy to monitor it daily, weekly, and monthly to see if our marketing tactics are working.

In other words, see if the plan for achieving the goal is executed as it is established. Our benchmarks are MS(Market Share), Sales, and Profit. You must have all three.

when the management uses commissions for sales reps to increase sales. Incentives have to be 30% of the person's salary. One major side effect is that when there is no commission, there is little to no motivation for the sales rep to bring in revenue.

If sales and profits increase, but market share falls, there is no market growth. If MS(Market Share) is growing but there is no profit, then the pricing was established too low. If sales is stagnant that means that marketing has failed to reach new customers and increase indication.

It is the marketing team that works to address the above problems. Many marketing teams, however, do the job of sales support, including promotional work, paperwork, and statistical data generation. What is even more concerning is that they begin to believe that such administrative tasks are their job.

You should always check the purpose and direction of what you are doing. When the process is out of order, it goes downhill. Have MS, Revenue, and Profit increased today? You should see this for yourself and your team every day.

Don't forget that sales and marketing have distinctive roles.

Establishing
Market Price

Price sensitivity is weak in pharmaceutical sales. In the case of medicine, the state determines the price of the drug so the product, promotion, place, and price of the 4P marketing strategy will vary by state. The price of the original price determines the followers' prices. Late comer to the market sets prices at 80% of the original product. There is not much leverage on pricing for the late comers.

The cosmetic surgery sector that I've been in charge of is uninsured, therefore, pricing is not a significant factor. There are many concerns about how to set the price.

When a new brand is introduced,, the customers are unaware of the value of the products. The marketing is responsible for convincing the consumers to understand and accept the high price.

- Is the product quality good?
- Are the effects and results after the use of the product positive in the long run?
- Do many professionals in the field already use the product?
- Do you know all the brands that patients know about, even if you are not in marketing?

MINT, a product from HansBiomed, unlike competing products, received FDA clearance and is priced at three to four times higher than the competition. However, we were unable to confidently answer the last question.

Will our customers immediately agree with the

marketing points set forth by the company?

Although the higher the frequency of advertising and publicity, the greater is the recognition, the budget was limited, which limited marketing activities.

People ask for a lot of testimonials or expert opinions when buying a product.

We take this into account and make our marketing strategy to maximize the use of our products in each hospital. When clinics witness improvement in patients' conditions, they promote the procedure to other patients. Increase in consumer's marketing activity is a sign of successful marketing and high quality. The proof of its effectiveness in renowned hospitals and the fact that large hospitals are using our products instigate other hospitals to try our product. After that, questions about prices do not come up that often.

However, the emergence of competitors has led to a drop in prices. Despite our product being the original one, MINT was forced to lower prices due to the influx of competitors. When a competitor steps into the scene, what would be the correct pricing strategy? Most of the time consumers are willing to consider a new product if it is 20% lower than the existing product. They are willing to buy if the price falls below 80% of the original one.

The medical sector is more conservative than others. Thus, such price strategy on its own is not enough. In other words, it will take some time before the product becomes widely used. Doctors won't pay for products that do not have predictable outcomes. The effect is important, but if doctors think the safety issue is not yet guaranteed, they will withhold their decision.

BellaGel, the first breast implants produced and manufactured by Hans, was very hard at first launch. Moreover, less than six to seven countries can actually produce breast implants. however we have created a world-class product called "Smooth Fine," which is more qualifed and luxury brand than implants from Allergan and Johnson & Johnson. BellaGel Smooth Fine(SF) claimed presence claimed presence in the Korean market. The consumers were impressed by the quick responds to complaints, and the upgrades that followed. BellaGel Smooth Fine's pricing immobile at the moment.

What is valuable to the consumer, how it differs from others, and sufficient value constitute the power to maintain a high price. Setting prices is, of course, a complicated process, but I think that if I do my best to listen to market trends and spend a lot of time improving and developing products, I can get the price I want.

Consumers are sensitive to Q, P, and S(Quality, Price, and Service). It's tricky. Kazuyoshi Komiya[6] once said,

- - - - - - - - -
6 The best management consultant and CEO of 'KOMIYA consultant'

"I can go further and say that I'm grateful to have a competitor. Many times, the customer sees the combination of QPS and decides which company to choose. In other words, you need to have a competitor to help your customers compare QPS and realize their superiority."

The success of the pricing strategy depends on employees to deliver valuable brand image to consumers through sales and marketing. The five- and four-star hotels have different facilities, but the overall satisfaction from the staff's service differ the most. The friendly attitude of the staff in the halls and restaurants makes the difference. Although staying at a 4-star hotel is great, I would rather spend more money at a 5-star hotel treat their customers as honorary guests.

Definition of
Sales

I'm a CEO now and in charge of various departments, but my career began with a marketing team. I studied molecular biology, which is far from marketing. It helped me a lot to understand the mechanism of medicines, but because I was ignorant about marketing, I had to invest in studying more marketing principles at the company.

So when I started as part of the marketing team at Amore Pacific Pharmaceuticals, it was fun but also a lot of work. I had a lot of worries, and when I went to strategy meetings, I would keep questioning if my ideas were good or not.

But the hardest thing for me was that I couldn't figure out how my values were viewed. I wanted to get promoted fast, to be recognized, to get feedback from customers, and to solve any questions immediately.

I was very frustrated by the team leader, but I visited the customers and spent the nights working in the office. Since there is no definite scope in marketing, there is a lot of unknown ground to cover. On the other hand, there were many times when I didn't even tee off.

When I moved to Daewoong Pharm, I joined the sales department as a new employee and started again from the beginning. I wanted to know what was going on in the field, and I longed to resolve the frustrations that I experienced in marketing. I wanted to be evaluated for what I did.

In 2005, I approached an impossible account and succeeded in selling Daewoong's products.

I believe that everyone engages in sales activity, whether it's the President of the United States or the president of any company. You are essentially telling everyone to invest in you and buy things you represent. The marketing team is selling the sales team, the internal department is selling the idea that office-related departments should carry out their work, the sales team is selling to the customers, but internally, the marketing team is selling to facilitate the work. As such, we are doing business with everyone. Sales is not just about selling good; but it is selling a relationship. Sales comes from softening the hearts of the people to listen to your story. Everyone is engaging in salary apartment.

All activities that help you do what you want to do, or sell is sales. So to accomplish sales we have to accrue knowledge and fortify relationships.

So then, what can you prepare to perform in sales?

Although there are some exceptions, most of the

sales team is evaluated by the revenue they bring to the company. Revenue is dependent upon how close the company is the monthly, quarterly, and yearly goal. What is the number? Sales. What are the sales? It is the rate at which a company has achieved its target for the month, year, and quarter.

Sales teams, MR(Medical Representatives), and sales representatives are people who achieve the goals of the company and organization. To be good at sales, you need to be close to people, work well, have good relationships, and be good at studying products.

In determining whether you are working well or not with your sales staff, evaluate how specific your goals are. Rather than being good at cooking, it is about seeing if you have set a particular purpose.

In other words, to achieve this goal, you have to worry about new places, product usage, customer drop-outs, missed meetings, etc. Typically, 10 minutes before going to bed, figure out what percentage of what you've done that day is contributing toward reaching your target for the month. Make this your habit at the end of the day.

Chairman of Daewoong, CEO Yoon, once asked an employee, "Do you have $20,000 in your bank account?" and the employee responded, "no." Then CEO Yoon asked him again, "If your wife had a surgery and you need $20,000 urgently, can you get it?" and he replied, "Yes."

It was an important question. Amid urgency, "no" can quickly turn into "yes."

The idea is to put YES first and think that the goal will be achieved.

Sometimes sales people ask, "How do you do well?" It's a complicated and challenging story. To put it simply, sales is the act of identifying and approaching a GAP with a goal. That is why sales team's main objective should be achieving the targeted revenue Whom would you promote: Someone who thinks of numbers or someone who does not do so? Team leaders and business managers should be more sensitive to numbers and goals. Who will be promoted and compensated? That would be the employee who is most susceptible to goals and numbers. Peter Drucker writes in his book, '*Management*'

"*The organizational structure that directs the attention of people or units in an organization to effort rather than performance is unacceptable. Achievement is the purpose of every activity. We should increase the number of people who act as managers rather than professionals or competent managers and those who are measured by performance or achievements that are not management skills or professional abilities performance or achievements that are not management skills or professional abilities.*"

Essentials of
Sales and Marketing

Let's imagine that you are selling a car. Would it be easier to sell a luxury sedan or a mid-level brand car? A vehicle from a mid-level brand by no means is of low quality. Quality is essential for any company to establish it's the brand name. However, from the perspective of the customer, the luxury brand name carries more value than just quality.

From the seller's perspective, branding and quality are equally important. How good would a product be if it had all the desired traits? The opportunity to sell these products does not come often. Brand outweighs the quality at times.

I launched a company with the hopes of creating a high quality product that does not rely on brand image.

BNS and HansBiomed have more than 20 products registered and cleared by the US FDA. We promote products of proven quality that are safe and effective without relying on the brand image to draw in consumers.

A marketing campaign will undoubtedly increase budget spending. The more spending increases, the more customers will seek you, which then will require more expenditure. It becomes a vicious cycle, but having a thorough knowledge of the advantages and uniqueness of your product is the key to overcoming the cycle. When you can convey such knowledge to your customers, then the customers will begin to trust you. Their trust is the ultimate goal of marketing.

That is also the case with quality. The sales company must like the product. In your business, do you consider your products to be the best? Doesn't Elon Musk think that Tesla's cars are of superior quality and that he is good at sales? The future of sales will look different from what it is today.

The product must outshine the company. Over time, the reputation of the products creates the brand image; thus, we need to invest all our energy into the product.

Many domestic distribution companies and small companies, rely on imported products because these products are considered superior. But, will the oversea headquarters continue to rely on these smaller companies to distribute their products? They will soon want to sell directly to the market.

It is the role of the marketer to invest in the product features and collect testimonials on the benefits of the product. Then what is the purpose of sales? You should consult your opinion leader and understand why they should use your product and what makes them use the product. what would the doctors and customers want to hear from the salesmen?

Consumers are willing to listen to your sales pitch because they are looking for innovative tools to enhance their practice Once you have persuaded about 30% of them, you are off to a good start. Conveying them to convert to your offering may take years.

Once a KOL decides to use your product, their insight and know hows will enhance your working knowledge and instigate enrichment of the product quality. An intuitive leader will add a new indication that others didn't think of, and the product will have evolved one step farther from an infant stage.

The salespeople MR, marketing, PR team, sales planning team, executives, and the president are working towards one common goal, sales.

Preparing
of Successful Sales

What are the most critical factors in sales? Two key factors must be in balance; one of them is having in-depth knowledge of your product. I've witnessed a sales rep sell a product without an adequate understanding of what he was selling. Some reps are not even aware of the price changes. These reps should not be at the forefront of sales. You must have an understanding of what differentiates your product from a competitor's offering. Knowing the features of your product alone is not enough.

Why should customers buy and use your products? You should possess the answers to the following questions:

- What are your advantages, and how are you different from your competitors?

- What are the results after use (compared to other products or competing products)?

- What side effects are there? What is the instruction for aftercare?

- What are your disadvantages, and what can you offer to overcome the advantages of your competitors?

- What are the appeal points for marketing your product to my patients in hospitals and clinics?

Sales executives add their philosophy to what marketing has put together. An answer to just one of above mention is neither pervasive nor persuasive enough to approach consumers. You have to have an extensive, in-depth answer to at least two of the questions to transact a deal.

The phase of But even gaining product knowledge and meeting customers can be daunting. The best and the quickest means to solve a problem is to face it head one. A face to face encounter with the customer may be uncomfortable but will change the nature of the relationship between you and the consumer. customer. Physicians usually first come across our brand at conferences, seminars, or symposiums. The consumers of the medical device industry are innovative and fashionable in following the newest technology.

Consumers may be somewhat fashionable. However, they still start to get curious about the product by listening to the stories of key opinion leaders (KOL), decision-makers, and people who hold sway over the opinions of specific groups. You shouldn't sell the product cheaply or trust it to an employee who doesn't have product knowledge. When we go to buy a product, why don't we think not only of the people but also of the product if the staff selling the product is not professional? The knowledge of the employees who are at the forefront of selling the products is what makes the company, refined and fabulous.

In this way, the customer listens to the real story of choose the product.

The key to human relationships is to think about how to benefit our customers. In other words, explain politely and in a straight forward manner, the reason why the customer should use the product will help the customer.

For customers to use the product well, all employees must inform and persuade the characteristics of the product not only to doctors but also to patients.

Being polite and kind is fundamental. You have to be an employee who contemplates a strategy to help the hospital grow in sales. This mindset is the beginning of healthy human relations.

There is no priority in product knowledge and relationships. Both are important to balance. Rather than biasing one of them, the two must always complement each other. Competitive products continue to pour, and relationships don't forever flourish.

To be an expert at what I do, I have to work every day. It is vital to maintain relationships once you have established them. If you neglect the visits as you've been doing, your competitors will have more visits to your target customers.

The 1:1 encounter is still necessary, but large hospitals demand better marketing, such as product characterization and differentiation. As a result, companies have become increasingly concerned about changes and emphasis on product strategy. In other words, the marketing team is tasked with opening doors to societies, symposiums, seminars, etc. to make sales departments more easily connected, along with studying how to reach the target audience better.

Building trust with the two most important components of sales: valuable products and relationships, leads to the final step of networking by introductions to other customers. After about one or two years of operation, if you have gained enough trust and earned a reputation, the customers will introduce you to other potential users.

The time comes when my work and efforts change from quantity to quality. After years of building up potential, more introductions occur your way, and the very thing that was difficult at first becomes easier.

Meeting customers is the job of the salesperson. Many salespeople ask, "Why did you support your sales?"

Of course, sales are the people at the point of contact with the customer. However, the short-distance athlete who competes in the Olympics prepares for four years and runs for about 10 seconds at 100m. It takes years of exercise and four years of preparation, but the result shows in just 10 seconds. Sales are 90% preparation and 10% execution. Results are an accumulation of 90% preparation.

How many customers do you expect your MR to meet in a day? If you meet two or three people a day, you have met a lot. A visit to a customer is called a call. For a pharmaceutical company, the standard requires a salesperson to make 20 calls, and it is ten calls for a medical device company. After the first encounter with the MR, the customer thinks one or two more times and decides whether to meet again or not. It's similar to a blind date, with 80~90% of the first meetings deciding whether or not to meet again. The first meeting may be the last.

I tell my staff that I am always 90% ready. In other words, don't try to meet often, and when you meet, you need to be prepared to do more. Then what can you prepare in advance?

All the work starts with a list. List all the client accounts in a spreadsheet. Then search all relevant information regarding the accounts.

It's not about your product; it's about helping the hospital. Talking about the products or related topics you are interested in will make the atmosphere more comfortable and, of course, end in more consultation time. There will be a moment when your needs align with the needs of the consumer. It is important to list up all this information beforehand.

Secondly, after the list-up, we look for common denominators in our product and hospital client specialties. The sorting process starts after the list-up.

In our company, we match the frequently used products in the hospital, such as BellaGel Breast implant, MINT PDO lifting Thread, and human tissue BellaGell with those listed.

This is classified as Category 1, and Class 2 is classified by characteristics such as customers with similar lines, customers with similar visit times, and large hospitals or small and medium hospitals.

The first step is listing, the second is sorting, and the third is projecting a goal for each account.

Each account has a purchase capacity. As a salesman, your job is to estimate the minimum and maximum potential purchases. You can only arrive at estimation after multiple visits to the office, and you also cannot manipulate the capacity of the clinic. One would assume that mega clinics with vast patients would have higher capacity. However, this is not always the case; smaller clinics that focus primarily on one specialty may make a purchase.

In other words, it follows STP(segmentation, targeting, positioning) in marketing. The priority is probably a hospital with a lot of CAPA even though you may have several competitors.

After listing, sorting, and evaluating the CAPA of the clinic, inspect what you have to offer. How will you approach the clinic, and how can you be of help to enhance their practice? A salesperson's mantra should not be "sell and sell," but rather, "what can I bring to the clinic, and how will it help enhance the service?"

This way of thinking makes a big difference. It is the difference between a good salesperson and an average salesperson. Some salespeople regard the consumers as revenue sources or those who consider them as families. In the past, Baek Seung-ho, executive director of Daewoong Pharm, has always emphasized that we must have a "mind for customers."

[Successful Hospitals]

- How my product benefits the hospital
- New products to increase hospital income and reputation
- Introduce product-specific indications to grow target audience
- Design, copy, concept, and advertising design for marketing and promotion of hospita

---

The above should be organized and prepared. In particular, share some of the strategies or content that other customers have used to bring about the success of their products. Consumers are more likely to welcome you if you share tips that would benefit as well as helpful product knowledge. The important thing here is never to talk about hospital names. We shouldn't be gossipers.

Importance of Managing Team

The sales force is at the front lines and interacts with the customers. In a war, they would be the gunmen, but they are not the gun makers.

Sales management and planning teams are management teams that check and evaluate how well things are doing on the sales floor.

In other words, non-sales departments such as the accounting team, sales planning team, human resources team, sales management team, marketing team, marketing support team, online team, offline team, design team, public relations team, etc., will help the sales team take off and land safely.

All departments are interdependent, and basically, all groups are involved in making sales.

First, the marketing team watches the sales trend and sees if the sales are doing well, the sales of the leading products and new products, the distribution of sales, the sales by the significant account hospitals. The team monitors and analyzes aggregate data on whether or not policy and strategy are lagging. Marketing teams should provide this data to their sales managers, presidents, and executives to help them plan their future strategies.

What about the sales planning and management team that monitors any breakaways, problems, or abnormal transactions, and ensures that there are no problems with logistics, delivery, etc. They prevent any issues that may appear.

The HR team helps new and experienced employees

settle into the company comfortably after they join. They also monitor the company's rules and well-being for its employees, ensure that employees have adequate benefits, and in particular, provide them with ongoing training opportunities to lead their work more efficiently.

We know that everything we do is connected. There are companies with strong sales teams, marketing firms, or internal departments, but they also interconnected with each other.

The sales team doesn't carry out menial tasks at the company, but it has the most critical role. This team brings in the revenue for running the corporation. But the company can't do it with the sales team alone. How the non-sales management team leads the sales team is just as important. The department that tells you how to get to the final destination the fastest and with the least effort is the management department.

In the field of sales, of course, the problem at hand is often severe that we often don't see the big picture, and the management team has to objectify the information to let them know where and how the business is now. Management should not be flexible. It is a team that listens to everyone but adheres to the principles. Sales are where flexibility matters, and you want to generate sales even if you have to break the policies. If you follow every policy, transactions can be challenging, so your team leader and boss are always in a dilemma.

However, the policies should not be compromised if short-term profits can cause problems in the long run. The company's principles must be a standard that customers can accept. The company's progress in violating the security principles, credit, payment method, payment deadline, and delivery of the goods of the company may be all right in the short run. In other words, sales that go off track do not produce good results. Even if your sales aren't doing well at the moment, it's better to look at them in the long run and build healthier sales forces.

Medical Sales vs. Pharmaceutical Sales

I have worked in many medical sales sectors. I started my career in pharmaceutical sales at Amore Pacific, where I stayed for four years before moving on to Daewoong for ten years. At Daewoong, I also worked in medical device sales with the DN company, a subsidiary of Daewoong. Then with my own company, BNS, I delved deeper into the medical device world. My career path ultimately led me to HansBiomed, which specializes in biologics and medical devices.

A pharm sales rep must obtain enough knowledge to converse with the doctors. Such knowledge is the basis for developing a product differentiation strategy to distinguish a product from similar offerings on the market. Customers will begin to trust the salesperson if his or her information carries validity and integrity. Once trust is there, the customers will be more open to making a purchase.

With so many generic products, even the original offering requires a differentiation method. For instance, Pfizer monopolized the market for medication for erectile dysfunction with Viagra when it held the patent. After the patent had expired, other companies were eager to come up with a generic version. The companies that manufacture generic drugs must aggressively develop and accentuate the differentiating points.

Major pharmaceutical companies such as Merck and GSK build the brand around the quality of their products. Customers associate the brand with the guarantee of quality and trust the value of the name. Salespeople play a more significant role when the provisions of competitors are balanced. The persistence and hard work of the salesmen may become the determining factor in closing the deal on sales. Such circumstances may be especially true when the customer has not established brand loyalty. Imagine yourself at a shoe store, and you are deciding between Nike or Adidas, and you do not have a preference for either brand. You are more likely to base your decision on the recommendation of an informative sales associate. The ability of the sales associates to deliver helpful guidance in purchases is just as important as the brand name and quality of the product.

Then what about medical device companies?

Some pharmaceutical companies launch a medical device division under the illusion that sales will increase if their salespeople work hard. It's not that you don't need a salesperson, but you need to understand the key. In addition to product knowledge and human relationships, medical devices have important considerations: securing KOL(Key Opinion Leader).

For example, surgery fees vary by hospital. In the case of non-insurance, the price range varies a lot. University hospitals, etc., may be similar because they put an upper limit on the cost. Still, in the case of uninsured medical care, such as cosmetic services, the operating expenses are different and vary by the size of the hospital and or by the surgical equipment used. However, most of the price depends on the experience, history, and reputation of the surgeon. Some hospitals are bound to perform well and also have good results. A major medical device used by an exceptional doctor could have a near 100 effects even if its potential is limited to 80-90. If the medical equipment is capable and the doctor's skills are excellent, is it not the icing on the cake?

If an inexperienced salesperson directly explains the correct and incorrect indication of a product, communication with doctors will not go well. Therefore, sales representatives of medical devices should not sell their products but should rely on KOL to communicate with the new doctors on the products they sell. "Salesmen cannot sell. Only doctors can sell."

If the KOL's clear and correct surgical method is delivered, and if other doctors agree and comprehend the accurate surgical technique for the product, then the product will be sold. This type of mechanism applies to medical device sales.

Discovering these KOLs and growing them together is the main task of the president of the company and the marketing department, and it is the job of sales to handle them efficiently and integrate them with the targets.

Running Your
Own Start Up

Many aspire to become entrepreneurs, and I, too, had the same goal. After working at Amore Pacific and Daewoong Pharmaceuticals, I started BNS and became an entrepreneur. HansBiomed eventually acquired BNS after four years. In the four years that I headed up BNS, I learned invaluable lessons.

Reaching the milestone of one million dollars in sales seems easily attainable, but only 4% of ventures reach the benchmark. At the time of its acquisition, BNS was making five million won in revenues. Along the way to its five million marks in sales, I realized that everything takes three times more than initially estimated.

If you estimate that reaching a benchmark would take three months, it will most likely take nine months. There are too many diversions along the way and very little assistance. In an organized corporate setting, there are many sources to draw help from, but such support is no longer available when you are on your own. You will also be spending three times the estimated amount in the capital. For the first two years, likely, you won't see a profit and will have to rely on intial capital until your business becomes profitable.

The core components of a business are its product, people, capital, and system. It takes time and experience to strengthen the core. You have to continually evaluate them: Is the product competitive in the market? What differentiates it from competitors? Is my marketing effective? Customers are now more knowledgeable than ever. If the product is not up to par, then consumers will not return. It's more beneficial to have input from the KOL than to attend multiple trade shows. Assigning and allocating budget for marketing activities is another vital factor. You may find yourself spending too much on ineffective marketing.

In the early stages of business startups, the president should not just leave the marketing to the people below—he should instead think about doing it himself. In particular, employees coming from more prominent companies often lack practical experience.

There are so many risk factors, including the arrival of competitors, along with the intensifying rivalry in the market. Not surprisingly, startups are more vulnerable to crisis.

So how much effort should it take? It is not clear how profitable or detrimental it would be without professional knowledge of finance or accounting, so be prepared. The establishment of BNS served as the foundation for my current position as the CEO. Also, the time at Daewoong Pharm was a time when I got a taste of what it means to run a company. These are the "beginner days" that equipped me to face off the competitors.

Everyone wants to run their own company, especially when individuals are already stressed while working for a company that you do not like.

The reason I started my business was to ensure my retirement goals. In any case, with an ordinary salary, salary men's future after retirement is rather bleak.

If I am the president, I do not have to worry about what will happen after retirement. In particular, even if I worked 3 to 4 days instead of 5 days and received a small salary, I would still be happy knowing that there was something that I could do, like sharing my accumulated knowledge to those around me. There are a few critical components of running a start-up. You need a product, workforce, system, passion, and, most importantly, investment. The invaluable experiences that I gained while working in different positions were essential in this operation. However, I was not prepared to handle fiscal issues.

The investment amount is three times more than the projected amount, but the cash flow is also three times slower. All costs are about three times higher than anticipated. Whenever anyone is thinking of establishing a start-up, I advise them to prepare for added expenses.

BNS had the fastest growth rate among all the medical device companies, and it still does. Now, HansBiomed has acquired BNS and has become an affiliate of HansBiomed's domestic sales division. We are becoming a dependable company with capital and products. What I felt while starting a business was that I had to multitask in all areas and do it earnestly. In particular, it seems to be true that less than 10 billion SMBs are responsible for 90% of their performance.

There will be times when you don't like your boss's work, don't like the work of my colleagues, and don't like coworkers. But remember these are fleeting emotions. "If things don't work, I still have a backup plan. Many do not pour out their burning passions. Paid employees indeed may not. It's natural to have a different position and idea, but when you find a boss who has the same passion as you, you should aspire to become an executive yourself."

As for the company's performance, 90% was my effort, so there was no one else to blame. When there is an employee, I am unhappy with, I hold myself responsible for working with my vague ideas and plans.

I initially had a hard time managing and maintaining inventory. I wasn't able to properly handle issues such as out-of-date products, products that had to be thrown away at the wrong storage temperature, bar code errors, and first-in-first-out items. Through the process, I had to change staff and team leaders three times. In particular, we were close to losing millions of won in inventory every quarter.

Then I realized the problem. I thought, "Do I know the real problem?" As Stephen Covey said, I was instructed not to let others understand what I did not understand. When I was in charge of inventory management, I knew that I had to understand it so employees could follow along. Then I had to be honest and discuss what the real problem was.

Kōnosuke Matsushita once said,

"If you are struggling in an organization or company, you must tell them the full truth so that everyone in your organization can have the right mind, the right mind."[7]

Running a startup may have been the most challenging

----

7 Kōnosuke Matsushita was a Japanese industrialist who founded Panasonic, the largest Japanese consumer electronics company.

task yet a most rewarding and fulfilling thing. It's good to get promoted in the order of manager, director, managing director, or president, but I also think it's good to be a boss and to be a managing director. The managing position will give you a better understanding of your job. The language of the boss is not the language of the employee but the owner. Think of yourself as a master. I've practiced this, though that might not have helped me a bit as HansBiomed's president now.

Effective Claim Handling

Sometimes, a customer makes a claim. There are many different types of packaging, such as changing information and not delivering information, damaged items, or near the expiration date.

The key is that within 12 hours, the claim must be clearly received, and all issues related to the product should be communicated to the laboratory and production department to avoid secondary issues.

If the delivery must happen by noon, How many days will the delivery take? What kind of card is interest-free? There is a lack of a channel for delivering results.

It's also a matter of integrity. Not fulfilling what is

promised, such as not delivering the advertised materials, service materials, etc., is a sign of a lack of integrity.

Timing is of the essence. A pro golfer knows the perfect timing and impact required to control the shot. Similarly, in sales, there is an ideal time for achieving the most impactful sales.

If you don't know what's essential and don't know the urgency of doing it, why not try doing it this way?

There is a "4, 3, 2, 1" rule. Make visits four times per week in the beginning, then continue with fewer visits each week, until you come to make a single visit in the fourth week. Lighten up your face at least once a month.

Moreover, only accurate information should be delivered. For example, a stamp should be applied on the spot, so that we accurately communicate the data of our products to the doctors, employees, heads of staff, nurses, etc.

I recall a pleasant experience I had in buying a luxury watch at a duty-free store. The watch was pricey, and I contemplated it for a year before making the purchase.

The pre-order duty-free shop in Korea allows you to shop before your date of departure and pick it up on the day of your flight. The exchange rate at the time of my first visit was 1,140 won for 1 dollar. I hesitated to purchase the watch because of the reduced exchange rate, so the manager of the shop promised to update me on the currency rate, and he kept true to the promise. He updated me whenever there was a drop in the exchange, and after three updates, I purchased the watch at a much lower exchange rate. His persistence and consideration were very impressive and reinforced the trust I had in the brand.

Sales is not a one-time transaction. You must listen to the customer's needs, consider what solution you can provide, and continue to build on the trust by following up on your words.

Use the claim as a channel to communicate frequently with the customer and leverage it to build a stronger relationship with them.

Medical Representative's Philosophy

Medical sales are different from sales of other industries in that the relationships start with the first order. An MR must make frequent visits to the clinics and invest in maintaining relationships with the users. Most medical professionals are loyal to the products if they feel that the product offers safe and compelling deliverables.

What factors trigger a purchase? We tend to conduct extensive research before buying a product. It's not very often you buy a product from a brand unfamiliar to you. We gravitate towards a brand that we know and trust. For instance, if you have been using an Apple phone, you will most likely seek out another apple phone when looking to upgrade to a new phone because you are familiar with this brand. Many people quickly dismiss products from unknown brands.

In medical sales, the brand needs to become recognizable. We promote our brand through symposiums, seminars, and marketing activities. When the user becomes aware of the brand name and becomes familiar with it, he will be more open to hearing about the products.

Each product offered has a specific purpose. Some products come to life from the requests of customers. There is no product made without a cause. Thus, the product has a unique identity, even if the product is a 'me too' product or a generic brand. It will have different features from other offerings of the market and was created to provide a solution to an issue or a need of the users.

MR is responsible for matching the needs of the customer to the product that can adequately address them. Customers are purchasing a solution. Competitive pricing is not enough to attract customers. An MR should consider what additional deliverables he or she can provide for the customers after a purchase. Most MR make the mistake of focusing solely on initial investment and neglect to follow up on how the products are used at the clinics.

To make repurchase happen, an MR must keep track of the inventory and how the clinic is marketing the product. The revenue accrued through repurchase is a big part of sales.

Most MR do not have a grasp on the three-months sales trend of the accounts. If a clinic purchased 100 units and only used ten in the first month, a MR needs to quickly asses the capacity of the clinic and devise a plan to help the clinic promote the item.

To do so, a MR should have data on the purchased vs used. It's burdensome for a clinic to hold inventory, so it will appreciate when an MR can help manage the stock. Inventory management is an essential factor, even in sales.

Don't wait until the end of the month to collect such data. I advise you to assess and analyze each account's needs and haves at the beginning of each month and quarter. How can you predict the next order without knowledge of usage data of the previous order? If a clinic does not place a new order when you project them to, your sales activity is not complete. Your job as sales is complete when a customer introduces you to another user, or repurchases according to your projection.

Our job as MR is to ensure that the products are being properly and safely used on the patients. New accounts and new purchases deserve praise. However, an increase in sales, satisfaction, repurchase from an existing account is even more noteworthy.

Epilogue

You probably have experienced the confusion of first love. In the first few years of my career, I was confused and unpolished as I was when first in love. When I reflect at that time, I do not remember much of those years. All I remember is that I worked hard but without a clear direction. I had an assumption about how the corporate world worked, and I was proven otherwise and left confused and defeated. Perhaps the first few years felt more arduous because I didn't have mentors to teach me better ways to do specific tasks and provide constructive criticism.

Most junior level managers probably didn't receive much guidance as entry levels and therefore lack the knowledge to train and advise the new hires. When the junior levels are unsure, they are more likely to get in conflict with the new hires.

How many managers can guide the professional development of the entry-level while relaying the core value and philosophy of the company? An amateurish manager can be a burden on other employees.

It is quite frustrating to work with new hires. I'm often left feeling drained from training them without results, and the work they produce is often insufficient. However, we, as a company, cannot neglect them. Entry levels may also favor being untended, but they are mistaken. What they learn in the first few years as new hires are the foundation for their professional life.

The first three years of job should sum to three words: Positive attitude, passion, and learning.

First, be positive and enterprising.

"Stay strong and stay positive." Workplace attitudes influence every person in the organization. Believe that you are capable of everything. Positivity begets positivity; There is power in a positive attitude, so things will work out as you believe.

Second, have passion.

Youth is not measured by age, but by passion and curiosity. Curiosity and enthusiasm are the privileges of youth. When children stop being curious, they stop pursuing their interests.

What I ask of the new hires is to have excitement for their work and give it all that they can. As an entry-level, pursue your career wholeheartedly and find joy at work. You enjoy games and hobbies because they are of interest. Make work your interest and pour out your passion into the action. When you love what you do, it's so much easier to enjoy everything else around you.

There will be work that you want to run away from; tend to it for six months and give it all you can before walking away.

Third, be ready to learn.

You may only receive seemingly menial tasks. The company will not entrust you with high risk work until you have built enough experiences. If you want to stand out, make your menial tasks seem indispensable. If you invest a little more effort into such assignments, you will see higher results.

You will find the answers when you focus.

On the weekends, seek out and seize educational opportunities provided by different agencies. Find out more about topics related to work such as international business, tax, perhaps even a third language.

The higher you move the corporate ladder, the less time you will have for yourself. So what you learn in the first three years will be the strengths and skills for the rest of your career. Consider your workplace as a school where you can learn while being paid.

Pat Mesiti writes in his book "*$1 Million Reason To Change Your Mind*"

"This doesn't mean that you should live life in a constant state of frustration, dissatisfaction, and disappointment, never being able to enjoy or appreciate what you have. No, like the athlete who is always pursuing his or her next 'personal best,' there should always be a desire in us to grow, to increase, and to go one level better."

I want to reemphasize that your key to success is not your degree but your mindset of a millionaire. Mark Twain believed that schooling was different from education and learning, "I never let my schooling interfere with my education."

Your Success Depends On What You Believe That You Are Capable Of Becoming. Find your strengths in the workplace and what kind of skills you offer that others can't make yourself truly valuable.

I wrote this book to mentor you through the challenges of the working world. I believe that it is vital for the new hires to navigate in the right direction through their jobs into careers. As you read through this book, I hope that the experiences and insights I gained through my career help you find the answers.

In closing, I would like to thank my wife, who has continuously supported me through the rigorous work schedule and numerous business trips, and friends and family for encouraging me to write this book.

Publisher's Epilogue

There is a famous saying that success depends not on the speed but the direction at which you move through life. I believe that this quote addresses worries about the workforce of this contemporary society. One may wonder, "how do you find the direction?" What are the secrets of successful people? Can I learn those secrets?

This book is a compilation of successful habits that the author has learned in his career. I would even say that this book is a manual of lessons for entry-level, junior manager, and even executives. It offers tips from the expert on medical device sales, as well as fundamental knowledge for any employee.

As you read through the sincere yet passionate advice from the author on work strategy to a personal relationship, you will start to gain an overview of the direction of your path. The vital key to success includes extreme self-discipline and a genuine passion for work.

In a hectic, fast-paced world, I hope that this book will help you navigate on the path towards success. May this book become a mentor for the workplace and a companion for the journey through a professional career. Do not lose courage and walk confidently with an armor of knowledge found in this book.

Above all, let this bring you a burst of positive energy and cast away all your stress.